Alan Swingewood is Lecturer in Sociology at the London School of Economics and Political Science.

The Myth of Mass Culture

The Myth of
Mass Culture

ALAN SWINGEWOOD

Lecturer in Sociology
London School of Economics and Political Science

HUMANITIES PRESS
Atlantic Highlands, New Jersey 1977

© Alan Swingewood 1977

First published 1977
in the U.S.A. by
HUMANITIES PRESS INC.
Atlantic Highlands, N.J.

Printed in Great Britain

Library of Congress Cataloging in Publication Data

Swingewood, Alan.
   The myth of mass culture.

   Bibliography: p.
   Includes index.
   1. Mass society. 2. Popular culture. 3. Socialism and literature. 4. Communism and culture. I. Title.
HN15.S955   1977   301   77–4699
ISBN 0–391–00699–1

Contents

Introduction

This book has grown out of a much larger and more comprehensive study of the problems of class domination in modern capitalist societies and especially of the question of the role of the state in the maintenance of the capitalist mode of production. In recent years there has been a remarkable revival of interest in Marxist theory and Marxist schools of thought. The major trend has been to rediscover the works of Lukács, Korsch, Gramsci, Adorno, Marcuse, Horkheimer, Rosdolsky, Benjamin (most of whose major works were written during the 1920s and 1930s) and counterpose them to both Stalinism and Trotskyism. At the same time there has emerged a contemporary Marxism which, grouped round the theory of structuralism and the work of the French communist philosopher Louis Althusser, strives towards a scientific methodology and a rejection of the 'humanist' basis of these older Marxists. In general, both this rediscovered and contemporary Marxism are philosophical, epistemological and abstract in orientation rather than sociological, concrete and historical. It is this elimination of the historical dimension in Marxist social theory which is perhaps the most striking characteristic of these different writers (with the exception of Gramsci), and·in their analysis of modern capitalism they develop a static and pessimistic concept of the social formation. To understand these different Marxist traditions it becomes essential to relate them to the historical and political contexts, especially to the failure of proletarian revolutions in western Europe during the 1920s and 1930s and the totalitarian nature of Stalinism: by 1940, with the murder of Trotsky, all effective opposition to Stalinism within both the

Russian Communist party and those parties outside Russia had been wiped out. Two fatal consequences resulted in the sphere of social theory and it is these which are examined in this book.

1. Marxist thought, which remained independent of the Stalinist Third International (1928 onwards), rejected the revolutionary role of the European working class, and in the work of the Frankfurt School (Adorno, Horkheimer, Marcuse, Kracauer, Lowenthal) the goal of socialism was transformed into mere utopia. Writing in the late 1920s and 1930s, during a period of titanic class struggles in Austria, Germany and France, the Frankfurt school argued that capitalism in Marx's terms was now an anachronism: massive state intervention in the market, the autonomous and reifying role of technology and science within the mode of production and administration, and the growth of a consumption-oriented working class had rendered the Marxist concept of class struggle obsolete. Modern capitalism was a mass society in which the proletariat constituted an atomised rather than an organised structure and was easily swayed by irrational ideologies such as fascism: in Western capitalism as well as in the Soviet Union the same processes were taking place, leading to a society of pliant and obedient masses. All independent and autonomous groups and individuals were either absorbed by the state or simply annihilated. In outline, therefore, the theory of mass society and mass culture identified with the Frankfurt school was worked out long before the Nazis sent their leading theorists into exile to America, where they developed a more *sociological* approach under the rubric of the 'culture industry'. Thus the working classes were the prisoners not only of irrational psychology and ideological disposition (supporting 'authoritarian' political parties) but also of omnipresent forces of the capitalist mass media.

2. This totally pessimistic vision of the evolution of capitalism and socialism was closely linked with perhaps the greatest illusion of orthodox Marxist thought: the belief in the historical necessity of capitalist decline from a progressive high point in the mid-nineteenth century to its degeneration

and virtual collapse by the 1920s and 1930s. For the Frankfurt School, the decline of capitalism was shown by a progressive weakening of bourgeois authority and values leading to problems of legitimation; for the Stalinists and for Trotsky also, capitalism would inevitably collapse through the workings of certain economic and social laws and the activities of a disciplined revolutionary party.[1] Capitalist culture and social relations must of necessity degenerate into barbarism or, revitalised by revolutionary praxis, form the basis of a socialist society. A theory of economic determinism and historical fatalism was thus characteristic of both the orthodox and the unorthodox Marxist analyses of culture: the forces and relations of capitalist production are brought into conflict and no further development is possible. Capitalist culture is therefore 'in decline', its social and ideological function to dupe the masses into false beliefs and bourgeois values. For many contemporary Marxists, the term 'late capitalism' implies that the historically necessary collapse of capitalism has been averted by the conscious ideological and cultural manipulation of the bourgeoisie over the proletariat.[2]

It will be the argument of this book that capitalist economy and technology and capitalist culture, far from degenerating into 'barbaric meaninglessness' (Adorno and Horkheimer) and irreversible decline, have achieved new pinnacles of economic and cultural richness and diversity on a scale unparalleled in human history: as there is no 'final crisis' in capitalist economy so there is no final crisis in its culture. Far from it: the development of the capitalist mode of production has served to augment, not destroy, civil society. It has created a more complex and autonomous social structure in which the key institutions of trade unions, political parties, occupational associations and the communications and cultural media are not dominated by a massive and all-powerful state apparatus but exercise a greater mediating influence than was ever possible during the 'progressive' phase of capitalist evolution. Capitalism has succeeded in building up and strengthening the social relations of production and working-class organisations so much so that a far more delicate balance of forces is now capitalism's most characteristic feature. Yet for those Marxists working in the shadow of the Frankfurt School or a dogmatic Trotskyism, contemporary capitalism is a society in which a totalitarian state intervenes decisively in the management of economic affairs by controlling the independence of the labour movement through a mixture of welfare programmes and the involvement of trade unions in governmental administration. Such monolithic concepts of social structure, however, cut short the dialectical movement: of course the modern state grows in size and complexity, but as capitalism strengthens the sphere of direct domination so it necessarily creates the basis of a powerful civil society. For as a dominant class the bourgeoisie must subjugate the proletariat to its authority and confront the daily realities of class struggle through the repressive apparatus of a strong, centralised state; but equally the bourgeoisie seeks to dominate society through its own institutions built upon parliamentary democracy and a free market economy and thus achieves legitimation not through force but through consent. But this process of hegemony is never total: as civil society grows ever more resilient with the development of independent bourgeois institutions, working-class organisations and socialist ideology come to challenge bourgeois-class domination. The exercise of hegemony within the context of contemporary capitalism (which in sharp contrast to nineteenth-century European capitalisms has successfully eliminated residual feudal, non-capitalist and non-industrial structures) has thus become centred on the mode of integration of the proletariat, especially in terms of politics and culture. This function of social integration (that is integration from above) is not carried out by the state: it is a process based on the complex relations between the private institutions of civil society, bourgeois ideology and working-class organisation and leadership.

It is not only the Marxists, however, who have argued for the collapse of civil society and thus cultural vitality: in the writings of literary critics such as T. S. Eliot and F. R. Leavis, a nostalgic longing for a pre-industrial, non-capitalist society functions as moral touchstone for their critique of modern industrial capitalism. For these writers, as with the Frankfurt school theorists, the bourgeoisie is incapable of creating cultural vitality: it is capable of creating only a pallid, mechanical 'life-denying' civilisation – society and its culture are in rapid decline. As will be argued in the first chapter, this particular theory of mass culture is based on a rejection of the capitalist mode of production as a revolutionary force which builds simultaneously the institutions of popular culture (such as mass media, journalism and publishing) and the material, technological foundations of a potentially democratic culture (such as libraries and educational facilities). In both the dogmatic Marxist and the literary/cultural theories of mass culture, the concept of culture itself is abstracted from the complex web of social relations within capitalism and transformed into a monolithic notion of 'culture as a whole'. Since in these theories both culture and society are disintegrating, the focus is entirely on this abstract notion of culture rather than on the specific determinations and the historically concrete forms of capitalist culture: the result is a crude 'consumptionist' theory of culture in which subjective judgement and moral evaluation dominate to the exclusion of scientific analysis.

In the third and final version of the mass culture theory examined in this book – cultural pluralism – the emphasis shifts almost entirely from questions of domination, legitimacy and cultural vitality to the more prosaic problems of who consumes 'what, where and how'. In this theory, culture becomes synonymous with *that which exists* at the level of everyday life and stratified consumption patterns; the broader question of the relation of culture to class domination and ideology disappears. The pluralistic theory of mass culture focuses on a non-problematic concept of social integration and takes for granted the question of legitimation. Culture thus becomes separated from ideology and the analysis of the values it expresses is never related to class and social structure.

All three theories are profoundly conservative in their social and political implications. A mass culture is not the same as a democratic culture for the institutions of the former must work against the democratic participation of the masses in political, economic and cultural activities at all levels of the social formation. Mass culture implies the existence of superior groups who take the important decisions on behalf of the others, an élite, or élites, who work for the people over the people. In this book I shall try to show the anti-democratic animus of these different theories all of which, in favouring a static, ideological concept of culture either rooted in or forced upon a largely passive mass, reject culture as praxis, a means of transforming the world through consciousness, action and values.

Chapter 1

The Theory of Mass Society

In George Gissing's novel *New Grub Street* (1891), two representatives of the new world of mass publishing are cynically discussing the profitable living and potential fortune which await them if they transform the semi-popular paper *Chat* into *Chit-Chat* and the serious *Tatler* into *Tittle-Tattle*. And why? Because the late nineteenth century is the age of mass democracy and universal semi-literacy: 'I would have the paper address itself to the quarter-educated ... the great new generation that is being turned out by the Board schools, the young men and women who can just read but are incapable of sustained attention. People of this sort want something to occupy them in trains and on the buses and trams ... what they want is the lightest and frothiest of chit-chatty information – bits of stories, bits of description, bits of scandal, bits of jokes, bits of statistics. ... Everything must be very short, two inches at the utmost; their attention can't sustain itself beyond two inches. Even chat is too solid for them: they want chit-chat.'[1] In almost identical language, a modern critic writes of the 'shapeless sprawling and anti-human' environment of modern mass society in which peo-

ple 'read manic journals and magazines' as they journey to the
'meaningless tasks' of work to find relief only 'in office flir-
tations, pin-up and pop-singer cults, film and television talk,
cosmetic and fashion preoccupations'.[2]

The culture of modern capitalism is thus defined by the
literary imagination as egalitarian and mediocre. Mass culture
'mixes,   scrambles   everything   together,   producing   ...
homogenized culture. ... Mass culture is very democratic; it
refuses to discriminate against or between anything'.[3] Thus the
inexorable levelling of culture and loss of standards: capitalist
culture and its artefacts become commodities, their function to
entertain, divert and reduce consciousness to a state of total
passivity. This chapter will explore the development of the
theory of mass society and culture in the pessimistic versions
associated with literary critics such as F. R. Leavis and T. S.
Eliot, and the Marxist critics T. W. Adorno, Max Horkheimer
and Herbert Marcuse as well as in the more optimistic and recent sociological theory of post-industrial society.

Origins: de Tocqueville, Nietzsche, Gasset, T. S. Eliot and Leavis

The historical origin of the concept of mass society is linked to
the rapid industrialisation of west European capitalism during
the latter half of the nineteenth century which created the social,
political and ideological conditions necessary for the emergence
of modern class society with its basis no longer in the notion of
the 'people' but in the *mass*. The development of the capitalist
division of labour, large-scale factory organisation and commodity production, densely concentrated urban populations, the
growth of cities, centralised decision-making, a more complex
and universal system of communications and the growth of
mass political movements based on the extension of voting
rights to the working class are the ideal characteristics of mass
society. But this term 'mass' also implies a change in ideology:
as pre-capitalist social relations dissolve in the wake of these
massive economic and social changes, the emerging bourgeois
ruling class seeks to legitimise its domination through the secular
and rational ideals of democracy, equality and material justice.

From a system of stratification based on hereditary privilege and rigid hierarchies of power and status, capitalism transforms social relations into those of formal egalitarianism: 'class' replaces 'rank', reason supplants tradition as the new dominant class seeks to subordinate to its authority both the residual feudal strata (aristocracy especially) and the nascent proletariat. The term 'mass', therefore, emerges within social thought before the ascending bourgeoisie has consolidated its power within the modern capitalist state. It is employed pejoratively by pro-aristocratic, anti-capitalist ideologues against the values and practices of commerce and industry.

The *theory* as distinct from the concept of mass society was developed during the latter half of the nineteenth century and was increasingly used to refer to the industrial proletariat. Its emergence thus coincided with both the economic ascendency of the bourgeois class and the emergence of the modern working-class movement and socialist theory. The first theories of mass society are thus defences of the dominant political class (whether aristocracy or bourgeoisie) against the democratic spirit of the subordinate strata, and the reassertion of rigidly defined social hierarchies in which decision-making remains the prerogative of élites. These social theories reject those democratic principles of government enshrined in bourgeois philosophy and revolution which they identify with cultural and social mediocrity.

Alexis de Tocqueville's *Democracy in America* (1835-40) has often been cited as the first sociological critique of mass society. Certainly Tocqueville appreciated the revolutionary implications of bourgeois ideology and the emerging socialist opposition to capitalist society. Thus he writes of modern society as no longer governed by hereditary principles and traditional ties of dependence but rather by an all-pervasive egalitarianism which breeds individualism, materialism and social instability. The industrial revolution is held responsible for 'the democratic disease of envy' and those economic and political theories which prove 'that human misery was the work of laws and not of Providence'. Tocqueville's critique of modern society is resolutely aristocratic. He argues, for example, that 'high culture' is threatened by the monotonous and routine nature of life in an industrial society, breeding a literature in which authors strive 'to astonish rather than please and to stir the passions more than to charm the taste'. The writer becomes a purveyor of commodities: 'Democratic literature is always infested with a tribe of writers who look upon letters as a mere trade'.[4] Tocqueville's identification of democratic ideology with social and cultural levelling is echoed in the writings of many of his contemporaries, but it is in the work of Frederick Nietzsche that the opposition culture/socialism finds its most aggressive expression. It is no longer bourgeois values which constitute the main threat to modern society, and in *The Twilight of the Gods* and *The Anti-Christ* (1888), he develops his 'aristocratic' critique of mass society explicitly against the labour movement: 'I simply cannot see what one proposes to do with the European worker now that one has made a question of him. He is far too well off not to ask for more and more ... if one wants slaves, then one is a fool if one educates them to be masters.'[5] Implacably hostile to any form of egalitarianism, Nietzsche demands a rigidly hierarchical society based on 'a natural order' of castes:

> In every healthy society there are three types which condition each other and gravitate differently physiologically; each has its hygiene, its own field of work, its own sense of perfection and mastery ... the pre-eminently spiritual ones, those who are pre-eminently strong in muscle and temperament, and those, the third type, who excel neither in one respect nor in the other, the mediocre ones – the last as the great majority, the first as the élite.[6]

For Nietzsche, as with twentieth-century conservative critics such as T. S. Eliot and Ortega y Gasset, the threat to modern society comes *from below*, from the 'common man', 'mass man' who must be taught to know and accept his 'natural' place if traditional culture is not to be submerged by barbarism. High culture, writes Nietzsche, has its basis in 'a strong and soundly consolidated mediocrity' for whom happiness is merely the 'mastery of one thing, specialisation – a natural instinct'. The view that the survival and maintenance of high culture depend on 'mediocrities' strikingly anticipates the hierarchical and organic concept of culture – culture as a unified whole, a way of life – in the work of Leavis and Eliot. But for Nietzsche, the main problem is that the common man, the mediocre, are not always content with their allotted social status. They become too easily swayed by what he calls the 'socialist rabble . . . who undermine the instinct, the pleasure, the worker's sense of satisfaction with his small existence – who make him envious, who teach him revenge'.[7]

For Nietsche, then, the threat to 'high culture' (philosophy, art, literature and science) stems directly from the insatiable demands and ideology of a mediocre 'mass'. It is important to emphasise that these are themes common to both nineteenth-century and twentieth-century thought. J. S. Mill, for example, argues that the management of government and the framing of public policy must always be left in the hands of a minority (his 'wise men'), but he stresses that the untutored masses should be educated out of their apathy and philistine taste. Unlike Nietzsche and Tocqueville, Mill was the first important 'democratic' critic of mass society and of the threat posed to bourgeois institutions and bourgeois values by the uneducated industrial working class. Nietzsche's critique of mass society, however, is resolutely opposed to both bourgeois democracy and socialism, forces which undermine traditional authority and inherent patterns of inequality. Ortega y Gasset's *The Revolt of the Masses* (1930) develops many of Nietzsche's ideas, especially his implied critique of collectivism. Defining society in terms of 'superior' minorities and unqualified masses, Gasset dogmatically asserts that 'the mass has decided to advance to the foreground of social life, to occupy the places, to use the instruments and to enjoy the pleasures hitherto reserved to the few', and the result is quite simply 'the political domination of the masses'. European culture is now threatened by these new 'barbarians' of the middle and working classes who remain 'incapable of any other effort than that strictly imposed upon them as a reaction to external compulsion'. Liberal democracy, built upon the rapid expansion of scientific and technical knowledge, is simply a vast mass of primitive, uncultured and atavistic mediocrities, their lives no longer informed by the civilising influence of traditional culture but rather by the pragmatic values of modern technology.[8]

The growth of science and the increasing role of the state in regulating modern society are Gasset's main points. The political element in the theory of mass society emerges only with the twentieth-century writers: Tocqueville and Mill assumed a *laissez-faire* function for the state, but with Gasset and T. S. Eliot (in his *Notes Towards a Definition of Culture* [1948]), the trend towards a collectivist, mass society is perceived as the direct result of the egalitarian social and economic policies adopted by democratic government. Like Nietzsche and Gasset, Eliot advances the view that since all known human societies are stratified into different orders, it becomes essential that the top stratum possess a more conscious culture than the others so that society resembles 'a continuous gradation of cultural levels'. Eliot's concept of culture is organic: the culture of every individual flows from his membership of specific groups and classes and these in their turn depend for their culture on the whole of society; culture, therefore, is a way of life and every society enjoys some form of common culture; each national culture is made up of many local cultures thus creating both diversity and unity within the whole. Eliot thus defends the myth of a static, organic culture against the 'barbaric' tendencies of the welfare state and mass media and, like Nietzsche and Gasset, sees the necessity for working-class institutions and ideals, especially those of socialism, to be assimilated by the dominant culture.

Eliot's main concern lies with the transmission and protection of this common cultural heritage; he argues that only a minority of a privileged élite can fulfil this role. For Eliot, families are 'the most important channel of the transmission of culture', and he warns that 'when family life fails to play its part, we must expect our culture to deteriorate'. Elites must, of course, remain closely attached to the upper class and thus discharge their function as the guardians of high culture. Equally important is the necessity for the political, artistic, scientific and philosophical élites to form a unified stratum. The traditional culture of a society is therefore passed on through generations of families and for this reason Eliot advocates that 'the great majority of human beings should go on living in the place in which they were born' for 'family, class and local loyalty all support each other; and if one of these decays, the others will suffer also'.

Like Nietzsche, Eliot defines modern capitalism in terms of unrestrained egoism and individualism, 'unregulated industrialism' which progressively weakens the moral bonds of a traditional common culture. It is a vision of society common to conservative thinkers and strikingly similar to Emile Durkheim's sociological concept of 'anomie', a state of normlessness brought about essentially through the decline of traditional modes of authority such as religion and the family. It is this crisis of authority within modern capitalism, the problem of legitimation, which forms the background to the development of the theory of mass society. The traditional governing élites can no longer rule in the old way: the bourgeoisie and proletariat now contend for political authority through mass parties and organisations.

Of course Eliot has no scientific grasp of capitalist social relations and class structure. He dismisses the middle class as 'morally corrupt', lacking 'independent virtues' and 'class dignity' yet strong enough to absorb and 'destroy' the English aristocracy. Thus surveying contemporary Britain, Eliot concludes that the social conditions necessary for the survival of culturally creative élites are disappearing and as 'one symptom of the decline of culture in Britain' he offers 'indifference to the art of preparing food'. More serious is the emergence of a society deliberately organised for the making of profits and, through the influence of advertising and mass education, 'the depression of standards of art and culture'. The working class, too, has lost its 'traditional culture' and with it its class vitality: the cinema especially has made the working class 'listless' while the mass production of gramophones and cars has simply reduced its 'interest in life'. Transmission of culture becomes the prerogative not of families but of the state; and this must be the death of traditional culture: 'We can assert with some confidence that our own period is one of decline; that the standards of culture are lower than they were fifty years ago . . .'.[9]

Eliot's critique of modern society is therefore built around the failure of capitalist institutions to create the kind of moral com-

mitment he associates with traditional religion. Mass society has
no moral centre, no universally accepted ethical code; industry
and materialism are by definition immoral because they are
profane and secular. It is this crisis of moral regulation which
lies at the heart of F. R. Leavis's concept of mass society.
Writing in 1930 in his *Mass Civilisation and Minority Culture*,
Leavis accepted that 'culture was at a crisis'; he then went on to
identify the main enemy as the machine: the arrival of the car,
for example, 'radically affected religion, broke up the family, and
revolutionised social customs' destroying 'the mature, inherited
codes of habit and valuation'. For Leavis, 'the present phase of
human history is ... abnormal' in the sense that there is no
longer a genuine 'common culture' with its moral assumptions
shared by all the people. Like Eliot, Leavis emphasises the
critical role which tradition plays in the life of a culture particularly for its development and basis in the 'organic community'. The pre-industrial world, he argues, allowed men to live
'as integral parts in the rural community' and as full members of
an 'old popular culture', 'a national culture' with its 'time
honoured ways of living' and the 'inherited wisdom of the folk'.
In 'Old England' both towns and villages 'were real communities', work was a meaningful not dehumanised activity;
there was no conflict between capital and labour and the
workers 'could, without a sense of oppression, bear with long
hours and low pay'.[10]

     Leavis's idealised sense of the past and his identification of
culture with a passive acceptance of an unchanging social world
and thus the hierarchies of power and inequality within lead him
to a complete rejection of the *technological* and *scientific* basis
of culture in the extended division of labour, industry and
knowledge which facilitate man's increasing mastery over nature
and society. To reject capitalist culture as a whole is to mis-
understand its contradictory development and to miss the
critical point of the potentially liberative qualities of modern
mass production and social relations. But for Leavis, mass
production and standardisation weaken man's emotional experience while advertising, radio and film impoverish his spirit.
Literature which sets out to distract has bad consequences:
romantic fiction, for example, is harmful 'in so far as a habit of

fantasying will lead to maladjustment in actual life'.[11] Modern culture has become an entertainments industry geared to 'passive diversion': in 1930, Leavis cites as an example Arnold Bennett, a contemporary best-seller whose work achieved critical acclaim only because there was 'no longer an informed and cultivated public'. The organic link between cultural (which for Leavis means the literary) vitality and the common culture is the essence of Leavis's critique of mass society. The decline of a 'living tradition' means the elimination of a mediating cultural stratum between the ordinary reader and writer. As will be argued later in this chapter, there is a close relationship between these ideas and those of Adorno, Marcuse and Horkheimer, cultural critics working within a totally different theoretical framework, but who, like Leavis, arrogate to the critic the task of resisting the inhuman processes of modern industrial society. Thus the absence of an informed, critical intelligentsia cultivating public awareness and appreciation of literature results in the isolation of creative writers from the broad mass of the people.[12]

The result is 'minority culture' and the necessity for an intellectual élite to maintain the cultural tradition:

> The minority capable not only of appreciating Dante, Shakespeare, Donne, . . . but of recognising their latest successors constitute the consciousness of the race . . . . Upon this minority depends our power of profiting by the finest human experience of the past; they keep alive the subtlest and most perishable parts of the tradition.[13]

As many critics have pointed out, there is here a tendency to define this minority in narrowly literary terms which excludes the scientific intelligentsia; equally, social relationships, indeed the quality of life in a modern capitalist society, are judged by this same literary criterion.[14] But in a sense this is unfair to Leavis: his main argument focuses on the crisis of values in modern industrial society and the decline of 'a coherent, educated and influential reading public'. The importance which Leavis ascribes to literary criticism in the creation and transmission of civilised values is bound up with his analysis of modern

culture as tending towards dehumanisation and a loss of community. The task of the critic is thus one of resistance against
the dominant tendencies of industrial society and to affirm the
central importance of human values, community and the common culture.[15]

Leavis's critique of mass society is almost entirely couched in
terms of a nostalgic return to an ideal, organic, pre-industrial
society; the modern factory worker, he argues, no longer prac-
tises a craft entailing 'the use of a diversity of skills' and containing 'a full human meaning in itself ', the products of his work
no longer serve a function 'in the life and purpose of a community that really *was* a community, a human microcosm, and
couldn't help feeling itself one'.[16] Yet Leavis is not blind to
historical change and he is thus forced to accept 'the
accelerating and inevitable change that was transforming our
civilisation'. His criticism is directed against mass publishing,
book clubs, newspapers and the mass media as agencies which
have undermined the organic relation between culturally creative
élites and a broad readership, for at the heart of his analysis is
the idea of culture as simultaneously popular and discriminating.
Leavis's emphasis on the essential link between 'life' as the common culture, the everyday experience of common people within
a morally binding community, and creative intelligence and
creativity distinguishes him from the arrogantly élitist theories of
Nietzsche, Gasset and Eliot. For Leavis, cultural vitality is
decisively threatened by the alienation of creative thinkers from
the common culture; for others, the collapse of the traditional
class system necessarily leads to fragmentation and sterility.

Mass Society as Totalitarianism: Mills, Adorno, Horkheimer, Marcuse and the 'Culture Industry'

Leavis represents the literary democratic élitist tradition of mass
society, the threat to culture stemming *from above*, imposed
through the profit-seeking capitalist mass media. Unlike this
cultural critique of modern industrial capitalism, however, the
sociological approach in its negative version is more concerned
with the fate of the potentially revolutionary working class in a
society 'ripe' for socialism. Ideology becomes of crucial impor-

tance for the values associated with the mass production and consumption of comics, pulp fiction and newspapers combined with the effects of television, cinema and radio corrupt and deradicalise the proletariat. Mass society is thus characterised as 'a relatively comfortable, half-welfare and half-garrison society in which the population grows passive, indifferent and atomised; in which traditional loyalties, ties and associations become lax or dissolve completely; in which coherent publics based on definite interests and opinions gradually fall apart; and in which man becomes a consumer, himself mass produced like the products, diversions and values which he absorbs'.[17] Traditional centres of authority such as the family become less significant as socialising agencies and 'individuals are related to one another only by way of their relation to a common authority, especially the state'.[18] Mass society is thus defined sociologically as lacking strong, independent social groups and institutions, a society dominated from above. And in the face of a world which appears beyond human control, man is resigned and passive, a prey to 'irrational' political movements such as Nazism and fascism. The manufacture of opinion by a centralised mass media affirms and buttresses these tendencies.

It is this emphasis on the manipulative function of the mass media, the exercise and mediation of power and control through the cultural 'superstructure' of society which distinguishes critics such as C. Wright Mills, Adorno, Horkheimer, Herbert Marcuse and many contemporary Western Marxists whose confidence in the revolutionary role of the industrial working classes has not survived their apparent integration into the culture of modern capitalism. The radical pessimism of this school of thought mirrors the conservative pessimism of Eliot and Gasset and the loss of confidence in *their* revolutionary class – the bourgeoisie – although these differences should not be exaggerated. Both traditions emphasise the drift towards a collectivist, totalitarian state in which all independent mediating social institutions have been progressively eliminated. This notion of a weak civil society is central to C. Wright Mills's *The Power Elite* (1956) in which the collapse of an informed and critically independent *public* into a largely apathetic *mass* is linked directly to the 'collective forms of economic and political life' associated with modern industrialisation: 'In brief, there is a movement from widely scattered little powers to concentrated powers and the attempt at monopoly control from powerful centres, which, being partially hidden, are centres of manipulation as well as of authority.' Although America is not yet a totalitarian state in the manner of Nazi Germany or the Soviet Union, the tendency is towards forms of centralised organisation and the complete destruction of primary groups and communities:

> The structural trends of modern society and the manipulative character of its communication technique come to a point of co-incidence in the mass society . . . segregating men and women into narrowed routines and environments . . . masses in metropolitan society know one another only as fractions in specialised milieux: the man who fixes the car, the girl who serves your lunch, the saleslady, the women who take care of your child at school during the day . . . . Sunk in their routines, they do not transcend . . . their more or less narrow lives. They do not gain a view of the structure of their society and of their role as a public within it.[19]

Mills's idealised and romantic view of past history links his critique with those of Eliot and Leavis while his fatalism and deterministic view of historical development echoes those of the culture critics of the Frankfurt School (Adorno, Horkheimer and Marcuse).* During the 1930s these writers witnessed the rapid rise of fascism and the total collapse of European Communism and socialism. It seemed that the forces of total reaction had seized the working class and that both liberal democracy and the labour movement were incapable of withstanding the power of unreason. For these critics an atomised social structure led inevitably to totalitarianism; fascism, far from being the political arm of monopoly capitalism, was increasingly analysed as a movement *from below*, from within the masses themselves.

---

*The Frankfurt School also included those who disagreed with the Horkheimer/ Adorno theory of mass culture: Walter Benjamin, together with Siegfried Kracauer and Bertolt Brecht, developed a more optimistic standpoint based on the possibilities of a new collective proletarian art (Brecht's Epic Theatre, for example) created by the collective nature of the capitalist mode of production.

For Adorno and Horkheimer, the central fact of capitalist civilisation was the progressive collapse of the family as an adequate socialising agency, its mediating function passing to 'the culture industry' – the purveyor of 'barbaric meaninglessness', conformity, boredom and 'flight from reality'. The term 'culture industry', first elaborated in Horkheimer's and Adorno's *Dialectic of Enlightenment* (1944) during their years of exile in the United States, was clearly intended to suggest domination from above although its success still depended on an amorphous, passive and irrational working class. The mass media are repressive: criticism of capitalism is stifled, happiness is identified with acquiescence and with the complete integration of the individual into the existing social and political order.

Two themes dominate the Frankfurt School's theory of mass society: the weakness of traditional socialising institutions in the face of massive economic and technological change; and the increasing reification of culture in which the objects of man's labour and activity are transformed into independent, autonomous forces seemingly beyond human control. The atomised man of mass society is thus ruled by 'blind necessity'. Indeed for Horkheimer and Adorno, the economic system of modern capitalism has become a self-regulating force dominated by inevitable economic and technological laws. Modern society, writes Horkheimer, destroys every vestige of the autonomy of individuals as it moves towards 'a rationalised automatic, totally managed world'.[20] Writing at a time (the 1930s) when the final collapse of liberal capitalist democracy seemed imminent, not in the way Marx had predicted but rather from the combined forces of totalitarian politics (fascism) and totalitarian economics (the growth of giant monopolies and cartels and the fusion of banking and industrial capital), the Frankfurt theorists became convinced that the evolution of capitalism necessitated the destruction of those social institutions – economic, political and legal – which, mediating between the state and 'civil society', had remained resiliently independent and provided some protection, however partial, against arbitrary political domination. Fascism destroyed civil society; every institution became politicised. In effect, Adorno and Horkheimer generalised from the specific development of German fascism to capitalism as a whole, arguing that the American 'culture industry' (a concept they preferred to 'mass culture' with its suggestions of spontaneous origin *within* the masses) performed the same functions as the fascist state. Thus Horkheimer's important study, 'Authority and the Family' (1932–3), on which Adorno and Marcuse (especially in the latter's *One Dimensional Man*) based much of their critique of modern capitalist culture, develops the argument that 'the psychic character of man' is determined by the stability or instability of major social institutions of which the family is pre-eminent. With the rise of modern capitalism, however, the family 'as one of the most informative agencies' in man's development loses many of its former independent functions. Linking changes in family structure with the crises and contradictions of society as a whole, Horkheimer argues that a decisive shift within the authority relations of the family has taken place. As a result, the family is transformed from a productive unit in which the father as its head 'was immediately seen in his productive social achievement' to the modern 'limited' type in which his position flows directly from 'the money he brings in' – a separation of work and home that must eventuate in an ideological and irrational paternal authority. It is thus through changes in the social structure that the individual becomes socialised into the virtues of obedience and conformity, learning to accept the social order as both natural and permanent; submission to authority within the family teaches equal submission to political and economic forces external to it.[21]

The isolation and collapse of the modern family was a common enough theme during the 1930s shared by many 'bourgeois sociologists', Marxists and literary critics such as Eliot and Leavis. Marx himself had written that under the capitalist mode of production the economic foundation was laid 'for a higher form of the family' and family relationships because production demanded that women and children as well as men work outside the domestic sphere; capitalism thus had the effect of attacking 'the economic basis of parental authority'.[22] Whereas Marx welcomed these developments as broadly progressive, Horkheimer and Marcuse identify them with the collapse of the autonomous individual. Unlike nineteenth-century capitalism, the most significant socialising agencies now are the state and technologically dominated labour. The result is the virtual elimination of all oppositional thought to the existing social order for, through 'a whole system of extra-familial agents and agencies' (ranging from pre-school gangs to radio and television), the ego is prematurely socialised: 'The experts of the mass media transmit the required values; they offer the perfect training in efficiency, toughness, personality, dream and romance.' The 'manipulated consciousness' of modern man thus means almost total ignorance of world affairs: 'The over-powering machine of education and entertainment unites him with all the others in a state of anaesthesia from which all detrimental ideas tend to be excluded.' [23]

In his essay 'Art and Mass Culture' (1940) Horkheimer extends these arguments to the sphere of culture suggesting that genuine art ('high culture') rather than reconciling the individual to the *status quo* − 'the plastic surgery of the prevailing economic system which carves all men to one pattern' − has always resisted the alienation and values of the dominant econ-mic and political order: 'Art, since it became autonomous, has preserved the utopia that evaporated from religion.' It is this transcendent, critical function that disappears with mass art, for with the rise of collectivist economies and bureaucratically controlled societies, the isolated nuclear family can socialise the individual only 'for his role as a member of the masses':

> The gradual dissolution of the family, the transformation of personal life into leisure and of leisure into routines supervised to the last detail, into the pleasures of . . . the movie, the best seller and the radio, has brought about the disappearance of the inner life.[24]

The individual is thus incapable of conceiving a social world different from his own and only in the works of the artistic *avant-garde* (Joyce, Picasso) does art remain loyal to him 'against the infamy of existence'. The products of mass culture, because they must appeal to a vast, homogeneous public, allow no scope for the imagination. They are an 'impoverishment of aesthetic matter' which, far from involving the reader in a genuine dialectic, conceive him as a passive object to be manipulated and controlled. In the fantasy world of the mass media, culture and entertainment are fused: mass art is 'a blind wallowing in wish fantasies' that must frustrate 'a normal emotional life' and educate the masses to obedience.[25] The Frankfurt theorists conclude by praising the 'conscious and active' nineteenth-century middle-class culture in contrast to the largely 'unconscious and passive life' of the modern, organised masses.[26] Art becomes a commodity lacking any real autonomy since it functions both to ameliorate the world of alienating work and as a mode of social integration following the disintegration of the family. In *Dialectic of Enlightenment* Horkheimer and Adorno argue that 'art renounces its own autonomy and proudly takes its place among consumption goods . . . marketable and interchangeable like an industrial product'. Leisure time, like work, is a 'forced activity' and 'amusement . . . the prolongation of work', a means whereby the alienated worker replenishes his psychological and physical strength to start work again. The 'culture industry' necessarily produces an art form dominated by a 'prearranged harmony', the absence of tragedy and the elimination of negative elements. 'Aesthetic barbarity', write Horkheimer and Adorno, becomes the essence of modern capitalist art, demanding from its subjects 'obedience to the social hierarchy'.[27]

There is, in these formulations, both an élitist conception of culture, the 'high' form acting as a means for transforming society through developing a critical consciousness, and a pessimistic dismissal of the working class as the too-willing victim of an overpowering reification. There is thus a close kinship of ideas between the 'Marxist' Frankfurt theorists and the reactionary Nietzsche: the masses are 'mediocre' and the bourgeoisie incapable of resisting the march of technological capitalism. If working-class action and institutions are thus impotent, what forces can save modern society from 'cultural barbarism'? For Horkheimer, Adorno and Marcuse the source of hope is resolutely idealist. In Marcuse's *One Dimensional Man*, for example, the Horkheimer/Adorno theory of art is linked with a total rejection of the Marxist theory of social change. The 'vamps, beatniks and gangsters' of contemporary commercial

mass culture embody the values of the existing social order: unlike nineteenth-century art, mass culture assimilates the potentially subversive, destructive and antagonistic content 'to a har-
monising pluralism'. Even the classics are not immune: produced and sold as cheap paperbacks on a mass basis, they 'come to
life as other than themselves; they are deprived of their antagonistic force, of the estrangement which was the very dimension of their truth'.[28] And as with mass-produced classics so
with 'light' music: 'A successful work of art', writes Adorno, 'is
not one which resolves objective contradictions in a spurious
harmony, but one which expresses the idea of harmony
negatively by embodying the contradictions, pure and uncom-
promised, in its innermost structure'. Popular music 'reconciles'
man to the *status quo*; the listener's role is one of total passivity.
Mass-produced music becomes an 'ornament of everyday life', a
depersonalised, collective and objectivised art form lacking any
'negative function'. Using the concept of 'aura' developed in
Walter Benjamin's important essay 'The Work of Art in the Age
of Mechanical Reproduction' (1939) Adorno argues that popular music, consumed and appreciated only by atomised
audiences loses that quality of uniqueness and charisma
associated with genuine art works. The 'decay of the aura'
within modern society is linked by Benjamin to the increasing
social significance of the masses, and the necessity to transform
art and cultural products into mass-produced commodities: 'The
film responds to the shrivelling of the aura with an artificial
build-up of the "personality" outside the studio. The cult of the
movie star, fostered by the money of the film industry, preserves
not the unique aura of the person but the "spell of the personality", the phony spell of a commodity.' [29] Thus jazz
converges with other stereotyped art forms such as detective fiction which, according to Adorno, 'regularly distort or unmask
the world so that asociality and crime become the everyday
norm, but which at the same time charm away the seductive and
ominous challenge through the inevitable triumph of order'.
Capitalism, Adorno concludes, reduces the individual to a mere
agent of objective social tendencies; only when an artist's work
is no longer 'suitable for immediate consumption, when it sets
itself against society, does it achieve significance'.[30] Even in his

later work after his return to Germany from the United States, Adorno holds firmly to his conspiratorial view that 'the culture industry intentionally integrates its consumers from above' through an ideology in which 'conformity has replaced consciousness' and where no deviation from the norm is tolerated: 'the total effect of the culture industry is one of anti-enlightenment . . ., that is, the progressive technical domination of nature, . . . a means for fettering consciousness. It impedes the development of autonomous, independent individuals who judge and decide consciously for themselves'.[31]

For Adorno, Horkheimer and Marcuse, then, mass culture forms the basis of modern totalitarianism, the removal of all genuine opposition to the reifying trends of modern capitalism. The most extreme statement of these ideas, one which gained notoriety during the 1960s was Marcuse's *One Dimensional Man*, a work which portrays the ordinary experiences of man in modern society in terms of 'false needs' that 'perpetuate toil, aggressiveness, misery and injustice', a social world in which work has become an 'exhausting, stupefying, inhuman slavery'.[32] In such circumstances, with the working class consciously integrated into contemporary capitalism, praxis becomes the utopian ideal of Marxist intellectuals; the genuinely negative and revolutionary opposition is confined to a privileged élite and a subversive art.

Mass Society as Pluralistic Democracy: Shils, Bell and Post-Industrial Culture

Reviewing the work of the Frankfurt School theorists, Edward Shils argues that their analysis and concept of mass society can be understood only in terms of a 'frustrated attachment to an impossible ideal of human perfection and a distaste for one's own society and for human beings as they were'. Caricaturing the theory that 'the masses don't read Tolstoy but comics', he nonetheless rightly attributes their pessimistic conclusions to the failure of the European Marxist movement in the face of fascism and consumer capitalism. Their critique of mass society, he argues, is nevertheless the result, not of European experiences, but of their exile in the United States:

Here they encounter the 'mass' in modern society for the first time. Their anti-capitalistic, and by multiplication, anti-American attitude found a traumatic and seemingly ineluctable confirmation in the popular culture of the United States. ... The same factors which lead ... to National Socialism are responsible for modern man's eager self-immersion into the trivial, base and meretricious culture provided by the radio, the film, the comic strips, the television, and mass-produced goods. It is therefore to be expected that the mass culture which has been created to meet the needs of alienated and uprooted men will further the process, exacerbate the needs and lead onto an inevitable culmination in Fascism.[33]

The Frankfurt theorists, Shils concludes, romanticise a mythical past, a stable and organic society that has now given way to a fragmented urban culture in which man is isolated, alienated and an easy prey to totalitarian politics. In sharp contrast to this radical pessimism, the 'progressive evolutionist' theory of mass society (adumbrated in the work of Shils, Daniel Bell, Riesmann's *Lonely Crowd* and forming an important element in the more recent theory of 'post-industrial society')[34] celebrates the greater scope for human initiative, development and freedom engendered by the emergence of industrialisation and technology; political democracy, rather than being threatened by these processes, is strengthened as the social bases of political pluralism are augmented. The emphasis is on the strength, not the weakness, of civil society:

A plurality of independent and limited-function groups supports liberal democracy by providing social bases of free and open competition for leadership, widespread participation in the selection of leaders, restraint in the application of pressures on leaders, and self-government in wide areas of social life. Therefore, where social pluralism is strong, liberty and democracy tend to be strong; and conversely, forces which weaken social pluralism also weaken liberty and democracy.[35]

The theory of pluralism, therefore, has a concept of modern

society based on an equilibrium of forces in which independent, non-inclusive social groups exercise a limited measure of democratic control through their access to the major élites. Society is thus a complex structure of checks and balances in which no one group wields dominant power; 'The intermediate structure of pluralist society helps to maintain access to élites by virtue of its *independence* from élites.' [36] In pluralist society, therefore, social life is enhanced, not impoverished, as the broad mass of the population for the first time in human history engages in a democratic mass culture: in the past a largely illiterate population read nothing and it was only a small fraction of the upper classes who participated in cultural activities. The emphasis within this pluralist, progressive evolutionist school of sociology, however, is not on the narrow, literary-artistic defini-tion of culture but on a concept which stresses its practical, social and political dimensions. An excessively romantic view of the past inevitably ignores or minimises the cultural potential of trade unions, educational institutions and working-class political parties. Such a view ignores the fact that, with rising educational standards and increasing leisure time and affluence, contem-porary industrial society creates conditions of high mass con-sumption: more and more people become 'skilled' in the art of consuming the products of 'high culture' as evidenced in the vast sales of paperback classics and classical records. Consumer capitalism, rather than creating a vast, homogeneous and culturally brutalised mass, generates different levels of taste, different audiences and consumers. Culture is stratified, its con-sumption differentiated. [37]

Mass society, therefore, is the result of pluralism and democracy: the progressive evolutionist concept of modern in-dustrial capitalism is one in which social integration flows naturally from forces within the social structure and is not forc-ed upon a pliant population through the agencies of a 'culture in-dustry'. Mass societies are thus 'aggregations of people who par-ticipate to a much greater degree in the common life and . . . comprise people whose attitudes, sentiments and opinions have some bearing upon the policies pursued by their governments . . . [they] are a creature of the modern age . . . the product of the division of labour, of mass communication and a more or less democratically achieved consensus'.[38] In defining pluralism in terms of mass society the progressive evolutionist theory shares with the Frankfurt school a rejection of capitalist society as a class society and a mode of production in which social relations are mediated by exploitation and the inequalities of power and wealth. The theory of post-industrial society is built around the concept of pluralism and a decentralised power structure, a 'participant society' in which the old ruling classes have been superseded by a classless stratum of intellectuals, scientists and managers whose ideology is one of 'professionalism', not capitalist profit; the 'logic of industrialisation' is such that the working class diminishes in size and the rapid growth of service industries creates a vast new middle class of white collar workers and technicians. Post-industrial society is a mass society to the extent that the old conflicts between capital and labour have ceased to have structural significance and scientific and technical knowledge has replaced private capital as the most important factor of production. It is a society which is democratic and fluid in its social structure, dominated by a common, middle-brow culture diffused through the agencies of the mass media, a culture no longer identified with a dominant ruling class: 'A fairly uniform pattern of mass media use is now common to all social strata in industrial societies, and judgements of what is "good" and "bad" have become blurred.' In post-industrial society, the 'educated strata . . . are becoming full participants in mass culture' and 'it seems now possible to conclude that . . . industrial society does have something like a common culture which is that provided by the entertainment media'. It is therefore no longer a question of ruling-class ideology or the exploitation of the mass by the few but of 'needs common to most members of industrial society and catered for in ways made possible by the technology of mass communications'.[39]

The post-industrial society theory with its emphasis on consumption rather than production does not deny the existence of corrupting elements implied in any mass-produced culture or the persistence of alienating tendencies such as delinquency, urban squalor and poverty but explains such features of mass society as the unintended and dysfunctional consequences of the industrialisation process. There is therefore no concept of a crisis of moral regulation which underpins the Eliot/Leavis theory of mass society and no problems of authority and legitimation. In general, the progressive evolutionist theory of mass society succeeds in eliminating the whole question of ideology and domination from the analysis: the new mass media eventuate in a democratic common culture which reinforces, not weakens, democratic institutions and processes. Thus, although the progressive evolutionists' rejection of the totalitarian nature of mass communications clearly separates them from the radical pessimistic school (Adorno, Horkheimer, Marcuse and Mills), their depiction of modern capitalist society in certain significant essentials (that is, a largely self-regulating economy in which technology has become the dominant element, a passive working class and a new middle class totally integrated into the social and political structure, authority and legitimation defined, if at all, as non-problematical and severed from all questions of property and ideology) is identical. In these two versions of the theory of mass society, class struggle has disappeared and consensus (forced and natural varieties), passivity and pluralism dominate social consciousness.

It would be misleading, however, to conclude that the optimism of the progressive evolutionists constitutes the only sociological theory of mass society. In the wake of widespread social conflicts, persistent high levels of unemployment, inflation and an increasing dissatisfaction with the quality of life in modern capitalism, there has now emerged a pessimistic version of the progressive evolutionist theory. As we have noted, the progressive evolutionists do not have any concept of a crisis of moral regulation and therefore no theory of legitimation. Thus, revising his earlier optimism, Daniel Bell has recently written that 'for the modern, cosmopolitan man, culture has replaced both religion and work as a means of self-fulfillment or as a justification ... of life' without, however, creating those civic values in the absence of which society must necessarily collapse into anarchy or anomie. The Protestant ethic and bourgeois work culture has been eclipsed by a consumer-oriented, post-industrial society dedicated to hedonistic individualism; the logic of egalitarianism has led to a 'revolution of rising entitlements' and a society in which material aspirations are no longer mediated by a binding moral centre. In such circumstances, 'the traditional institutions and democratic procedures of a society crack, and the irrational, emotional angers and the desire for a political saviour come to flood tide. The decline of liberal democracy . . . and a shift to the political extremes may well be the most unsettling fact of the last quarter of the century.' Thus this version of post-industrial mass society concludes with resolute pessimism: nearly fifty years separate Leavis's *Mass Civilisation and Minority Culture* from Bell's *The Cultural Contradictions of Capitalism*, yet how similar is their analysis and understanding of capitalist culture! Bell writes: 'The consumer-oriented, free-enterprise society no longer morally satisfies the citizenry, as it once did. And a new public philosophy will have to be created in order that something we recognize as a liberal society may survive.'[40] As will be argued in the following chapters, the problem of values and ideology in the legitimation of capitalist domination is central to the whole concept of mass society and the analysis of capitalist culture. The next two chapters will therefore discusss the relation of culture to class and the Marxist method for analysing culture; the problem of legitimacy and authority will then be analysed in the two following chapters in the context of the mass media and the realm of civil society.

Chapter 2

Marxism and Culture

Culture, Technique and Production: Trotsky's Critique

As we have seen, the theory of mass society and culture originated in those societies undergoing the rapid economic, political and social changes associated with the industrial and bourgeois revolutions. In post-revolutionary France and nineteenth-century industrial England, the old landed governing class gave way to the 'rising' bourgeoisie; the new dominant class attempted to impose its hegemony on the major institutions of civil society and ally all subordinate strata to its ideals and practice. In general, however, the theorists of mass society reject these hegemonic pretensions and identify cultural health and vitality with pre-bourgeois culture and traditions, emphatically repudiating the rationalist egalitarian implications of bourgeois ideology and revolution. There is thus a striking parallel between this conservative defence of the old culture and Marx's argument that, as the bourgeoisie necessarily revolutionises the economic and political foundations of capitalism, they create simultaneously the conditions for their own overthrow – the industrial proletariat, socialist ideology, revolutionary theory and mass political organisations. It is in this sense that the theory of mass society defines bourgeois domination as inherently unstable, not simply for the maintenance of 'old' standards but as a check to the 'vulgar' pretensions of the uneducated and philistine 'masses' raised to cultural prominence by the same forces which have liberated the bourgeoisie. Paradoxically, the Marxist theory of mass culture also develops partly as a defence of 'old' standards against the 'new' but more specifically as an explanation for the failure of socialist revolutions in the advanced capitalist countries. In this theory, the working class has been 'bought off', integrated into capitalist culture, no longer capable of either political praxis or generating a genuine oppositional class consciousness and culture.

The conservative implications of both types of theory are fairly obvious. What is far more significant, however, is that in all forms of the mass society thesis there is no theory of the relation between culture and the economic structure of society, especially the mode of production and the social relations of production. In the mass society or 'culture industry' argument, the concept of culture is severed from production in all but a general and superficial sense; culture is thus transformed into an independent, autonomous realm of human activity (or a lack of it) explicable in terms of its own norms and concepts. The link between culture and class formation, structure and ideology is blurred; culture is analysed in idealistic and ahistorical categories. Writing of Leavis, Lionel Trilling has put this point forcibly, arguing that, for Leavis, 'a class defines itself by its idea of itself – that is, by its tastes and style. Class is for him a cultural entity. When he conceives of class power, as he often does, it is not economic or political power but rather cultural power that he thinks of. It is true that cultural power presents itself to his mind as being in some way suggestive of class power, but the actualities of power or influence are for him always secondary to the culture from which they arose or to which they give rise'.[1] Leavis, of course, would be shocked at the suggestion of the class nature of culture and the idea that the dominant culture within each epoch is that of the dominant class and that culture is an instrument of class rule and oppression. For while it is true that, in a very general sense, culture is a collaborative activity embracing all sections of a population, it is equally true that culture can be a divisive, not unifying, force and in modern society one of the means whereby a dominant class legitimises its rule over the subordinate strata. Through the major social institutions (the family, religious, educational, political and trade union organisations), cultural values, norms and aspirations are transmitted, congealing into largely nonconscious routines, the norms and customs of everyday experience and knowledge. At the level of popular consciousness, culture is never simply that of the 'people' or region or family or a subordinate class. Culture is not a neutral concept; it is historical, specific and ideological. The issue here is both the concept and method of analysis: culture does not exist apart from its specific determinations in a social formation; culture develops in and through the many levels, or structures, of a society (economic, political, educational etc.), which form the totality of social relations and practices. An idealist, non-historical and abstract concept of culture will tend to eliminate the genetic approach to analysis, while the emphasis on the organic, collaborative character of culture will tend towards an uncritical idealisation of the past.

In contrast, the Marxist concept of culture focuses on its specific, historical determinations. As an abstraction, culture has meaning only in terms of class structure, economic system and political organisation; culture is impossible apart from the material means of production such as tools and machinery. It is industry, the specific mode of production, not art, literature, philosophy or religion, which determines the quantity and quality of cultural development. At the foundation of culture lies the material means for its production and reproduction: technology. Thus writing of the Italian artist Raphael, Marx emphasises that the development of artistic talent itself hinges 'on demand, which in turn depends on the division of labour and the conditions of human culture resulting from it'.[2] And in the *Grundrisse* (1857–8), after noting the dependent and uneven relation of culture to economy, Marx asks:

Is the view of nature and social relations on which the Greek

imagination ... is based possible with self-acting mule
spindles and railways and locomotives and electrical
telegraphs? What chance has Vulcan against Roberts & Co.,
Jupiter against the lightning-rod and Hermes against the
Crédit Mobilier? ... Is Achilles possible with powder and
lead? Or the *Iliad* with the printing press, not to mention the
printing machine? Do not the song and the saga and the muse
necessarily come to an end with the printer's bar, hence do
not the necessary conditions of epic poetry vanish? [3]

Engels, too, although in a more dogmatic spirit than Marx,
observed the technological basis of artistic culture by making
Homer's *Iliad* dependent on Greek metalworking, shipbuilding
and architecture.[4] But of all Marxist discussions of culture, it is
Trotsky who approaches a genuinely sociological standpoint.

His definition of culture stresses the active and class elements:
'Culture is the sum total of all knowledge and skills amassed by
mankind throughout all its preceding history .... The conjunc-
tion of the skills and knowledge of historical mankind ... of
nations and classes'.[5] Culture is not simply 'a whole way of life'
but grows out of man's active relationship with nature. History
and society thus become the *only* means, through science and
knowledge, of freeing man from poverty, ignorance and class exploitation. In sharp contrast, Leavis's conception of the organic
community with its inherent moral values suggests that the foundation of culture is not material production and technology but
religion. This idealist concept of culture thus opposes Leavis
(and Eliot) to those forces in the capitalist world, especially
science and technology, which generate a materialist or sceptical
outlook and thus work to undermine traditional values and
social organisation. Historically, as Marx and Engels emphasised in *The Communist Manifesto*, capitalism constituted a
revolutionary mode of production:

> The bourgeoisie cannot exist without constantly revolutionis-
> ing the instruments of production, and thereby the relations of
> production, and with them the whole relations of society.
> Conservation of the old modes of production in unaltered
> form, was, on the contrary, the first condition of existence for

all earlier industrial classes. Constant revolutionising of
production, uninterrupted disturbance of all social conditions,
everlasting uncertainty and agitation distinguish the
bourgeois epoch from all earlier ones. All fixed, fast-frozen
relations, with their train of ancient and venerable prejudices
and opinions, are swept away, all new-formed ones become
antiquated before they can ossify. All that is solid melts into
air, all that is holy is profaned, and man is at last compelled to
face with sober senses, his real conditions of life, and his
relations with his kind.[6]

Capitalism revolutionises politics, ethics and culture. Bourgeois
culture is thus necessarily opposed to the deeply traditional
culture of pre-capitalist society, which was profane in its
philosophy and even in its religious ideology. From the
Enlightenment onwards, the major bourgeois philosophers —
Adam Smith, Helvetius, Bentham and Mill — proclaimed the
secularisation of ethics and the pragmatic principle of utility as
the measure of the social world; capitalist culture opposes the
feudal residues of ritual and custom, attempting to impose the
prosaic material norms of precision and exactitude in place of
ingrained habit and tradition. The Protestant religion is peculiarly receptive to the self-discipline and restraint essential for
capitalist accumulation; as Marx noted, by transforming the
traditional religious holidays into workdays, Protestantism
becomes an important cultural element in the demystification of
the social world and the specific genesis of capitalism.[7] But for
Leavis, this kind of material practice is rigorously excluded from
the concept of culture as a whole way of life, as indeed are the
specific practices associated with the labour movement —
cultural and political activities born of the modern class struggle
and expressed through the collaborative and collective institutions of trade unionism and socialism. These are the major
practices of the nineteenth and twentieth century without which
no understanding of modern culture is possible. In essence,
Leavis's emphasis on 'folk' industry is an idealisation of feudal,
not modern, social relations and, as Raymond Williams has
noted, an attempt to attach humane feelings to pre-capitalist
culture, whereas the historical reality was of a hard and brutal

world dominated by illiteracy, superstition, servility, squalor and poverty.[8] To conceive the ideal of culture in a world in which few could read, where the technology necessary for the provision of a national library and an educational system as well as the means for the proper, scientific utilisation of agriculture and thus adequate food supplies were totally absent represents a callous and insensitive view of the past and a telling indictment of the literary idealist approach to culture. A high level of literacy and a speedy, reliable means of communication are essential components of a national culture; without modern factory production there can be neither schools nor libraries, only mass ignorance and superstition.

The abstract, ahistorical and idealist concept of culture is thus linked to a condemnation and rejection of those material and technological developments in communication which are essential prerequisites for a genuine universal culture, a real mass culture in which everyone can participate because each possesses the leisure, education and self-discipline necessary for material and spiritual advancement. Trotsky's comments on the cultural possibilities of the fledgling Soviet cinema are instructive in this context: 'the longing for amusement, distraction, sight-seeing, and laughter is the most legitimate desire of human nature. We are able, and indeed obliged, to give the satisfaction of this desire a higher artistic quality, at the same time making amusement a weapon of collective education, freed from the guardianship of the pedagogue and the tiresome habit of moralizing.' The cinema, he argues, is important both because it provides entertainment and as one of the most important instruments for 'technical, educational, and industrial propaganda, propaganda for sanitation, political propaganda, any kind of propaganda you please, a propaganda which is accessible to everyone, which is attractive, which cuts into the memory . . .'.[9] For the cinema, radio (and, today, television) compete 'not only with the tavern but also with the church'. They are the means of transforming those 'tenacious, psychological habits which come down from generation to generation and saturate the whole atmosphere of life', those time-honoured, ingrained customs which, operating at the level of popular consciousness and culture, embody and reflect hegemonic authority, the ways whereby the ideology of a dominant class (or 'rising' class) is transmuted into the prosaic routines of everyday experience: 'One might say that the richer the history of a country, and at the same time of its working class, the greater within it the accumulation of memories, traditions, habits, the larger the number of old groupings – the harder it is to achieve a revolutionary unity of the working class.' [10] The task of Marxist science is to challenge this cultural supremacy at all levels of the class struggle: the Marxist approach to culture is thus 'business-like' – knowledge and skills must be utilised for socialist ends and the development of socialist consciousness and praxis. Culture, writes Gramsci, 'is the organisation, the disciplining of one's inner self ... the appropriation of one's own personality ... the conquest of a superior consciousness whereby it becomes possible to understand one's own historical value, function in life, rights and duties'. [11]

Hegemony and the Theory of 'Incorporation'

Trotsky's arguments bear a superficial resemblance to those of the Frankfurt school, whose pessimistic conclusions are now widely accepted within contemporary sociological thought. Through the triple influence of bourgeois culture (especially the mass media), politics (extension of the vote and Social Democratic political parties) and bourgeois ideology, the working class has ceased to carry '*in itself* the power to be a class *for itself*'. [12] Indeed, far from constituting a revolutionary class, the working class of modern capitalist society has become 'deradicalised' through the workings of its own political institutions: 'Once the mass party of the underclass comes to endorse fully the values and institutions of the dominant class, there remain no major sources of political knowledge and information which would enable the subordinate class to make sense of their situation in radical terms'. [13] The failure of reformist Social Democratic parties to mount a decisive challenge against the dominant institutions and ideology of modern capitalism effectively eliminates the development of an 'alternative society' notion and opens the way for working-class consciousness to be so dominated by the prevailing 'value system' that even the act of voting for a Labour party becomes 'deviant'.[14] As for Marx's identification of revolutionary consciousness and praxis with 'the maturity of capitalist development', the opposite is the historical reality — that the working class is more 'likely to achieve a high degree of revolutionary class consciousness in the initial phase of the industrialisation process'. The process of capitalist development 'incorporates' the working class and its political organisations into bourgeois culture thus stabilising capitalist social relations: 'Social democracy . . . is the normal form taken by the systematic political inclusion of the working class within capitalist society.' Contrary to Marxist theory, revolutionary consciousness is not an inherent tendency of capitalism: it 'tends above all to characterise the point of impact of post-feudalism and capitalist-industrialism . . . .'.[15]

There is, finally, a 'Marxist' variant of these highly deterministic theories, one which seeks to emphasise the overpowering importance of the 'superstructure' for the processes of social integration. A dominant class, so this argument goes, exercises hegemony to such an extent that the 'ruled' class acquiesces spontaneously and passively in its own subordination and political impotence. Defining the British ruling class as a 'social bloc' welding together the aristocracy and the bourgeoisie, it is suggested that every major institutional and ideological structure is dominated by 'a social authority whose ultimate sanction and expression is a profound cultural supremacy'. This hegemonic class becomes the primary determinant of social consciousness, character and social customs, saturating civil society with the values associated with empiricism, utilitarianism and respect for hierarchy. Working-class institutions and culture therefore exercise no autonomy, the dominant, 'hermetic' culture of the ruling class effectively blocks 'the emergence of a universal ideology in the English working class'.[16] The English proletariat, formed before the development of Marxism, was thus forced into an 'innocuous and subordinate role', lacking in revolutionary ideas and organisation, its only coherent ideology that of Fabianism and Labourism, its own trade union and co-operative institutions and work culture incapable of anything approaching hegemonic leadership. This particular 'Marxist' standpoint is thus identical with the mechanistic sociological argument which locates revolutionary praxis only during the 'birth pangs' of modern capitalism: Tom Nairn is in no doubt that

> The great English working class, this titanic social force which seemed to be unchained by the rapid development of English capitalism in the first half of the century, did not finally emerge to dominate and remake English society. It could not break the mould and fashion another. Instead, after the 1840s it quickly turned into an apparently docile class. It embraced one species of moderate reformism after another, became a consciously subordinate part of bourgeois society, and has remained wedded to the narrowest and greyest of bourgeois ideologies in its principal movements.[17]

The working class, writes Perry Anderson, 'could not distance itself aggressively from society and constitute its own autonomous movement towards social hegemony'; the English proletariat thus forms itself into a 'corporate class':

> If a hegemonic class can be defined as one *which imposes its own ends and its own vision on society as a whole*, a corporate class is conversely one which *pursues its own ends within a social totality whose global determination lies outside it*.[18]

The problem with this particular formulation, as E. P. Thompson has noted, is that it inevitably defines only a ruling class as hegemonic, while a subordinate class is always corporate. Thus hegemony is reduced from a highly complex structure of social relations based on a mode of production to a monolithic notion of class consciousness which then becomes the major determinant of social integration. The Marxist theory of society as a totality comprising separate but interrelated levels which do not develop at the same tempo (the law of uneven development) and are thus partially autonomous has given way to an *essentialist* concept of the social formation as a homogeneous unity in which class structure and revolutionary consciousness are defined in absolute either/or terms.

This non-dialectical approach is characteristic of all forms of the 'incorporation' theory insofar as the contradictions within and between the burgeoning working-class movement and the institutions of bourgeois society are eliminated in favour of an evolutionary model of social development. To argue, for example, that in the early years of the formation of the working class a viable revolutionary potential and therefore an alternative culture could have existed is to be naïvely ahistorical. As Marx and Engels emphasised in the 1872 German edition of *The Communist Manifesto*, it was only with the rapid development of industry that a party organisation of the working class became possible and this class, for the first time in history, was capable of challenging capitalist domination. During the course of the nineteenth century, for example, the English working class built the strongest trade union movement in Europe and by 1900 had created its own independent political party, but its lack of political independence during the 'formative years' (1800–50) is perhaps the best indication that in the development of capitalist society the working class possesses neither the institutional culture nor the political ideology and organisation necessary for successful revolutionary praxis. In this sense the correlation made between the early phases of capitalist industrialisation and revolutionary consciousness is false although this is not to suggest that bourgeois society is never *threatened* by working-class political agitation and practice. As E. P. Thompson has shown, the English working class emerged as a potentially independent force in the forty years after 1790 when, rejecting the old forms of bourgeois radicalism, it began pursuing its own social and political ambitions. The rise of the working class

is revealed, first, in the growth of class-consciousness: the consciousness of an identity of interests as between all these diverse groups of working people and as against the interests of other classes. And, second, in the growth of corresponding forms of political and industrial organisation. By 1832 there were strongly-based and self-conscious working-class institutions – trade unions, friendly societies, educational and religious movements, political organisations, periodicals – working-class intellectual traditions, working-class community-patterns, and a working-class structure of feeling. [19]

As Thompson emphasises, the English working classes 'made' themselves: 'it was not the spontaneous generation of the factory system' the result of the external workings of the 'industrial revolution' on 'some nondescript undifferentiated raw material of humanity . . .'. Scattered in small workshops, not yet disciplined by a large-scale factory system, the working classes rebelled and fought for both democracy and their 'ancient' rights – the rights of free speech and personal liberty – culminating in the fight for an 'unstamped' press during the 1830s. These were working-class demands fought for by working-class organisations.[20] The emerging working-class movement stressed the values of collectivism, not individualism, mutuality, not competition, freedom, not repression: and in an England governed more through force than by consent, 'the central working class tradition . . . exploited every means of agitation and protest short of active insurrectionary preparation'.[21] The Luddite movement and the abortive Pentridge rising were the only occasions when the English working class took arms against an unrestrained and unregulated nascent capitalism. Yet, however much the Luddites are analysed as a revolutionary movement, its secret organisation and ideology failed as a direct challenge to state power: it could not be otherwise for, as 'a movement of *transitional* conflict . . . it looked backward to old customs and paternalist legislation which could never be revived; . . . it tried to revive ancient rights in order to establish new precedents'.[22] The most serious challenge to English bourgeois society came much later during the late 1830s and 1840s when the leadership of the growing working-class movement broke from the middle-class radicals and struck out for political independence. And this was possible only through the rapid development of working-class institutions (the general unions of the 1830s) and the awareness, for the first time, of a genuinely 'alternative' society based on socialist ideology and trade unionism.

At the advent of capitalist industrialism the workers were a *mass*, defined as a 'mob' lacking any political organisation and distinctive ideology; by 1840, the mass had become a class 'with its workaday ethos of mutual aid' reflected in trade unions, co-operatives, political unions and Chartist lodges and the decisive challenge to capitalist society and culture could come only from this source. The English labour movement, for example, achieved its political independence through the founding of its own Social Democratic party and, to a large extent, the class struggle has found expression through the reformist practices of trade unionism and labourism. This observation is of vital importance for it is essential to relate the historical development and specific forms of the labour movement and culture, not to such vacuous, ahistorical abstractions as the consciousness of the ruling class, but to the institutional structure of the capitalist social formation. Nineteenth-century English civil society was a classic example of bourgeois hegemony with its weak bureaucracy, strong Parliament, independent political parties and educational institutions; social cohesion and integration flowed from within these institutions so that 'reformism' became the necessary and progressive expression of the class struggle. The major institutions of the working-class movement − trade unions, trades councils, co-ops − developed after the decline of Chartism and especially towards the end of the nineteenth century. Such was the strength of bourgeois hegemony that, even with the extension of the franchise to the urban and rural working class, the trade unions identified their interests with the Liberal party. The miners, for example, usually taken as exemplars of class consciousness and militancy, were the last major union to affiliate to the Labour party and, in general, miners' interests were served by Liberal representation in Parliament.[23] There is little evidence that the English industrial working class could have developed a coherent socialist alternative to capitalism before the 1840s and that the growth of its own institutions, in itself, was capable of forging any alternative other than a utopian and reformist socialism. Socialist theory does not arise spontaneously from within the working class, only the institutional form of the struggle against capital: trade unions, co-ops and political parties must be seen in terms of their theory as well as class composition and culture. Equally, the concept of bourgeois hegemony does not imply that bourgeois ideology has penetrated every sphere of working-class life and neutralised every form of opposition. As capitalist society and the mode of production are complex totalities comprising separate levels which develop at differing tempos (for example,

industrial capital, finance capital; large-scale factory systems
with an advanced division of labour, petty-bourgeois business
enterprises; capital goods manufacture, tertiary and service industries) so each social class, based on the mode of production,
is formed out of distinct strata. Class formation and class structure develop dialectically with some sections more advanced in
organisation and ideology than others and therefore capable of
opposing the total penetration of bourgeois ideology into the
everyday life and culture of the working class. To be sure, this
process itself is complex and contradictory but the point must be
made that, although bourgeois hegemony and ideology can
block the growth of revolutionary consciousness and party
organisation, it does not follow that its impact on all strata
within the proletariat is identical. It should also be emphasised
that the concessions won by the working class from the
bourgeoisie *had to be fought for*, and that there is nothing inevitable about gradual social change which is the result of
working-class *action* and organisation against the interests of
the dominant class. As Marx pointed out, the English Factory
Acts which limited the hours of work and the age at which
children could legally be employed were the result not of
philanthropic intention but of class struggle:

> The creation of a normal working day is . . . the product of a
> protracted civil war, more or less dissembled, between the
> capitalist class and the working class. As the contest takes
> place in the arena of modern industry, it first breaks out in the
> home of . . . England. The English factory workers were the
> champions, not only of the English, but of the modern work-
> ing class generally . . . .[24]

A dialectical, not mechanical, nexus characterises the 'base –
superstructure' model of Marxism; the essence of social and
historical analysis lies in discovering the complex mediations
between and *within* economy and culture, consciousness,
ideology and praxis. To 'write off' the working class as a potentially revolutionary force is to acquiesce in those negative
theories of mass society discussed in the previous chapter which
tend inevitably to one conclusion – that the working class, as a

class, is incapable of its historic revolutionary mission; the aboli-
tion of capitalism is thus the prerogative of intellectuals and party organisations. In their 'Circular Letter' to the leaders of the
German Social Democratic party in 1879, Marx and Engels
emphatically rejected the view, then gaining ground in the German party, that the working class must subordinate itself to
radical bourgeois and petty-bourgeois leadership. To the leaders
of the S.D.P. (Bebel and Liebknecht) Marx and Engels were
quite specific:

> For almost forty years we have stressed the class struggle as
> the immediate driving power of history, and in particular the
> class struggle between bourgeoisie and proletariat as the great
> lever of the modern social revolution; it is, therefore, impossi-
> ble for us to co-operate with people who wish to expunge the
> class struggle from the movement. When the International
> was formed we expressly formulated the battle-cry: The
> emancipation of the working classes must be conquered by
> the working classes themselves. We cannot therefore
> co-operate with people who openly state that the workers are
> too uneducated to emancipate themselves and must be freed
> from above by philanthropic big bourgeois and petty
> bourgeois.[25]

At issue here is the question whether the working class is
capable of developing its own distinctive class standpoint at the
institutional and cultural level within the framework of
bourgeois hegemony. In his analysis of the 1871 Paris Commune, Marx was optimistic, arguing that the very concept of
Commune itself was something only the working class could in-
vent, 'fired by a new social task to accomplish by them for all
society, to do away with all classes and class rule, the means to
break the instrument of that class rule – the State, the cen-
tralized and organized governmental power'.[26] And in the
preface to his sociological questionnaire 'Enquête Ouvrière'
(1880) Marx urged that the French workers reply to it since 'only they, not any providential saviour, can energetically ad-
minister the remedies for the social ills from which they suffer'.[27]
But while the Commune represented the first historic form of a

workers' government with 'the people acting for itself by itself', it
was neither socialist in ideology nor in political practice. It constituted the highest organisation of the proletariat but lacked
overall socialist direction and leadership. Thus, although the
historical development of capitalist society is towards forms of
economic and political organisation at variance with the dominant bourgeois ideology of individualism and self-interest, it is
crucial to distinguish the form and content of working-class
collectivism and consciousness. The myth of workers councils
as the genuine mediators between revolutionary party and class,
the 'true democracy' which will serve as the basis of the socialist
state is a viewpoint which succeeds only in idealising the
proletariat and grasping the class struggle apart from its political
(ideological) determinations. Thus Gramsci, in his analysis of
the Italian Factory Occupations during the years 1919–20,
argued that 'the present period is revolutionary precisely
because we can see that the working class, in all countries, is
tending to generate from within itself, with the utmost vital
energy . . . proletarian institutions of a new type: representative
in basis and industrial in arena. We say the present period is
revolutionary because the working class tends with all its energy
and all its will-power to found its own State. That is why we
claim that the birth of the workers' Factory Councils represents
a major historical event – the beginning of a new era in the
history of humanity.' [28] But to see in workers councils the means
for creating a 'true and representative working-class democracy'
is to confuse organisational form with specific, revolutionary
content: during the years 1917–19, workers' councils in Russia,
Germany and Austria were dominated by the Social Democrats,
Mensheviks and Socialist Revolutionaries: the Austrian Councils, for example, were largely engaged in administrative tasks
such as the distribution of food and the organisation of welfare
while in revolutionary Russia the so-called 'conciliationist'
Soviets urged compromise between capitalist and working-class
interests.[29]

The question, then, of working-class culture is inseparable
from the larger issues of hegemony, bourgeois ideology and
socialist consciousness and practice. The 'incorporation' theory
assumes either a false antithesis between early capitalism and

revolutionary consciousness or postulates a working-class culture dominated entirely by capitalist ideology. Integration is thus a process brought about *from above* with capitalist values penetrating working-class culture, consciousness and organisation to the complete exclusion of other alternative values. But to work within the framework of capitalism is not to accept its values: hegemony is a form of consent wrought from a subordinate class precisely because the strength of civil society allows it to pursue its own ends through forging its own independent class institutions of trade unions, labour party and so on. At the heart of the incorporation theory, therefore, is a concept of a mass society dominated from above achieved by a 'forced' integration of the working class into modern capitalism. The development of capitalism necessitates the integration of the working class at all levels of the social formation since the essence of bourgeois domination is rule through the institutions of civil society (hegemony) and not the state (direct domination) and its legitimacy therefore depends increasingly on the active co-operation of the working class in working within a system for ultimate goals which are impossible to achieve within it.

Working-Class Culture, Bourgeois Hegemony, Class Domination and Ideology: Hoggart and Williams

But what is working-class culture? As we have seen in the work of Leavis, culture is approached from an idealist and ahistorical standpoint, one which ignores all problems of ideology and class domination. Thus, although Raymond Williams has described the question of working-class culture as 'the key issue of our time',[30] the tendency, at least in English cultural studies, has been to define culture in narrow social terms so that working-class culture becomes independent of political and economic institutions, inward-looking, self-enclosed and self-sufficient communities conceived as largely passive enclaves within capitalism generating their own distinctive values, institutions and practices. By divesting working-class culture of its historical basis in the class struggle and its relation with the dominant class and dominant ideology, a myth of a 'pure' working-class culture has thus evolved.

In what way is it possible to speak of a distinctive working-class culture, a popular culture built up and maintained through working-class values and institutions? Richard Hoggart's influential book *The Uses of Literacy* (1957) is one such attempt to identify the basic characteristics of working-class culture in terms largely derived from Leavis and the 'Common Culture' school. Following Leavis, Hoggart argues that a standardised mass culture is replacing the 'remnants of what was, at least in parts, an urban culture of the people'. Indeed, in his later writings, Hoggart maintains that a cultural classlessness is now developing and that '*Woman* is the first truly classless journal of the new Britain.'[31] This new mass culture, however, is 'less healthy' than the 'often crude culture' it is replacing. Hoggart defines working-class culture as the urban local culture of tightly-knit communities whose life experiences and expectations were reflected, fairly accurately, in working-class women's magazines such as *Peg's Paper, The Oracle, Miracle* and *Red Letter* in which heroes and heroines were portrayed simply as ordinary working-class people with whom the reader could easily identify:

> The girls are usually pretty . . . in an unglamorous way, in the way working-class girls are often very pretty. They wear blouses and jumpers with skirts, or their one dance-dress. The factory chimney can be seen sticking up in one corner and the street of houses with intermittent lamp-posts stretches behind; there are the buses and the bikes and the local dance-halls and the cinemas.[32]

Occasionally, of course, all this is simple wish-fulfilment, but Hoggart concludes by saying that 'the environment is that of most readers' and that these magazines have 'a felt sense of the texture of the group they cater for'.[33]

What, then, are the specific working-class values of these communities? According to Hoggart, working-class culture emphasises the importance of myth and ritual, and superstitious beliefs are often connected with health (for example, the length of hair and fringe medicine); there is a widely shared belief in fate and destiny and in the virtues of home cooking. As for intellectual culture – books, for example – the typical response is the negative 'What will it get you?' or 'What good will it do?' The texture of social life is one of gregariousness and sociability: in the family everything is shared, including personalities (our Jack); there is 'short-run hedonism', the immediate gratification of pleasures and a minimum of planning, or none at all, for the future. Money is not saved, life is unplanned, a mild hedonism pervades, 'one informed by a deeply rooted sense that the big and long distance rewards are not for them'. The attitude is 'Why worry? Keep on smiling.' This is the culture now threatened by the 'smart', 'slick', classless magazines and pulp fiction which are frequently American and full of violence, sex and sadism. American comics, unlike their British counterparts, are aimed at adults, not children, and the result is a movement towards a mass art which is simply a partial escape from reality, 'the pallid half light of the emotions' which must end by ruining all taste and a distinctive 'people's' culture.

Hoggart's approach to culture is highly selective and, from a theoretical standpoint, naïve and impressionistic. There is no awareness of the role of ideology in the formation of popular consciousness or of the relation between working-class community and the capitalist division of labour. Habits, customs and rituals, as Trotsky emphasised, constitute the basis of social order, the means whereby a subordinate class accepts its position in the class structure as natural and inevitable. Culture as praxis is eliminated in favour of culture as a complex of meanings derived from 'life as it is', culture as pragmatic adaptation to the existing society. In what way, therefore, is Hoggart's notion of a genuine culture of the 'people' a caricature or an accurate portrait of working-class culture? The magazines produced for the working class during the 1930s can hardly be said to form an organic part of working-class life, a genuine popular culture comparable with the institutional culture found in the trade union and co-operative movement. The products of capitalist publishing reflect bourgeois values, not working-class values: while it was true that the characters in the magazines were working-class in origin, as Orwell observed in his essay, 'Boy's Weeklies', the 'habits, insides of their houses, clothes, general outlook and speech' were middle-class; there was never any mention of unemployment, the dole, trade unions or politics. Misfortune was seen as individualistic or the result of someone's wickedness and never the result of the capitalist system; and while many of the stories were set in a working-class environment, there was no conflict of interests between capital and labour. Thus, while striving towards credibility, these magazines merely provided a way out of reality, they did not face up to it. All popular fiction, Orwell concluded, is 'censored in the interests of the ruling class', simply reflecting its ideology: the social world of the comic, for example, is non-socialist and blatantly chauvinistic.[34]

Hoggart's analysis of working-class culture focuses on the superficial aspects of working-class life, and his concept of culture is static and passive. The important point about culture discussed earlier in this chapter lies in its active, historical character: a broad, not narrow, definition portraying man's social practices, his values and meanings bound up with social institutions such as trade unions and political parties in which actions, ideas, values, and knowledge are fused into an organic whole or oriented towards some concept of an 'alternative' society. Unlike Hoggart, Raymond Williams offers a more radical approach although he follows Leavis and Eliot in defining culture as an organic, co-operative and collaborative activity. For Williams, 'culture is ordinary', and working-class culture is defined as 'a basic collective idea, and the institutions, manners, habits of thought and intentions which proceed from this'.[35] Like Leavis, Williams argues explicitly against the Marxist theory of culture in his suggestion that working-class institutions 'contribute to the growth of society' through their contributions to the development of a common culture. The problem with this formulation is that it tends to eliminate all those contradictions and conflicts of interest between and within social classes thus divesting the concept of culture of any role in class domination. Culture is thus transformed from a complex synthesis of specific determinations (political, ideological, religious etc.) into an essentialist and historicist concept. For to argue that trade unions express working-class values of mutuality and solidarity is to mistake form for content, since the dominant class also benefits from these characteristics in that class rule is impossible without cohesion and co-operation of the different fractions; collectivist values have meaning only in terms of ideology, consciousness and practice. Like Leavis and Hoggart, Williams rejects the concept of culture as ideology and fails to create any real connection between everyday experience ('culture is ordinary') and the mode of class domination, class formation and legitimation. There is thus no theory of hegemony, only a destructured and static model of society in which culture is defined in terms of meanings. In *The Long Revolution*, for example, he argues that 'the discovery of a means of communication is the discovery of a common meaning' which cuts across class interests; [36] and, in *Culture and Society* he writes that 'the human crisis is always a crisis of understanding'.[37] This subjectivist concept of culture is central to both Williams's early writings as well as to his more recent and avowedly Marxist works in that there is no attempt to explore the ways whereby 'cultural meanings' (or 'structure of feelings')[38] are implanted and how these relate to specific class interests. In short, Williams has neither a theory of social order and legitimation nor a method of analysis which might enable him to pose the kind of questions related to the problems of capitalist culture and domination.

The following chapter will explore the concept of working-class culture as it is rendered in fiction while subsequent chapters will explore in greater detail the relations of hegemony, communications, ideology and culture.

Chapter 3

Fiction and 'Proletarian Culture'

Marxism and the Concept of Proletarian Culture: Lenin and Trotsky

All dominant classes create their own distinctive culture. But the relation between culture and class is dialectical, uneven and contradictory and, as was argued in Chapter Two, while the development of culture is bound up with a specific mode of production, its division of labour and technology, culture is never a simple reflection or an epiphenomenon of these material forces. Bourgeois culture, for example, has a longer history than the history of the capitalist social formation, nurtured in pre-capitalist, feudal societies and maturing slowly over many centuries. This is why tradition is such an important concept for understanding the hegemony of a dominant class and the cultural subjugation of the ruled classes. In locating the industrial, urban proletariat as the 'bearer' of revolutionary consciousness and praxis, nineteenth-century Marxist theory assumed that the transition to socialism would necessarily generate a new and distinctive culture, a socialist culture in which the formal ideals of bourgeois ideology become transformed into the genuinely universal. Yet how was this culture possible? Bourgeois culture, for example, was the product of centuries, not the result of a sudden, revolutionary transformation of power: the proletariat, as a relatively 'new' social class brought into existence by modern capitalist industry, had neither the knowledge nor organisation to create a culture which would rival and negate that of the dominant class. The theory of 'proletarian culture', however, assumes the existence of specifically working-class values and practices which place the proletariat in the role of the hegemonic class *immediately after* the seizure of power. The socialist mode of production is immediately translated into a socialist culture.

The view that the proletariat could build its own *class* culture gained considerable support during the years following the October 1917 Russian Revolution. From within the Bolshevik party itself, a tendency and movement developed called the *Proletkult* which defined culture in simple class terms as a 'weapon in the class struggle' and an expression of 'pure proletarian ideology'.[1] Of those in the Bolshevik leadership, it was Lunacharsky and Bukharin who were sympathetic to the complete assimilation of culture to class ideology. In contrast, Lenin and Trotsky opposed the very concept of proletarian culture which they saw as inimical to Marxism. 'In reality', wrote Lenin in 1910, 'all the phraseology about "proletarian culture" is just a screen for the *struggle against Marxism.*' Lenin's point was quite simple: Marxism had absorbed the scientifically progressive features of bourgeois thought and culture in developing its political and social theory – but this was not to argue that Marxism *rejected* all previous bourgeois thought for, while Marxism represented a sharp break with bourgeois ideology, it was built upon the knowledge which the bourgeois class had made possible: 'Proletarian culture must be the logical development of the store of knowledge mankind has accumulated under the yoke of capitalist, landowner and bureaucratic society.' For Lenin, proletarian culture meant primarily the practical task of social and economic progress, of raising the appallingly low literacy and educational standards of the broad masses, and the development of agriculture, industry and technology. Proletarian culture did not mean the invention of theories of culture, 'not a dilettante self-admiring, Proletkultish so-called science ... but a serious education' lasting for years and involving millions of workers and peasants. As for the 'formal analogy' drawn between bourgeois and proletarian culture, Trotsky dismissed it with contempt:

> The bourgeoisie took power and created its own culture; the proletariat, they think, having taken power, will create proletarian culture. But the bourgeoisie is a rich and therefore educated class. Bourgeois culture existed already before the bourgeoisie had formally taken power. The bourgeoisie took power in order to perpetuate its rule. The proletariat in bourgeois society is a propertyless and deprived class, so it cannot create a culture of its own.[2]

Proletarian art and culture were mere fictions and could never exist precisely because of the temporary and transient nature of the proletarian dictatorship. For Trotsky, the 'historic significance and the moral grandeur of the proletarian revolution consist in the fact that it is laying the foundations of a culture which is above classes and which will be the first culture that is truly human'. Like Lenin, Trotsky saw 'proletarian culture' as the development of education, the growth of literacy and the general raising of cultural levels. Thus, although there is a close relation between culture and class, 'History shows that the formation of a new culture which centers around a ruling class demands considerable time and reaches completion only at the period preceding the political decadence of that class.'[3] The 'political decadence' of the bourgeoisie, however, has not resulted in proletarian revolutions in any of the advanced European capitalist countries and here the concept of 'proletarian culture' has come to imply a distinctive culture of a subordinate not dominant, class. And this is problematical: for in what ways can the working class develop its own ideology in a situation of bourgeois hegemony? Is there any such thing as a 'proletarian ideology' and therefore a proletarian culture? What are the values which distinguish 'proletarian ideology' and culture from the ideology and culture of the dominant class? This chapter will explore these problems in the context of that tradition in English fiction which has made the modern proletariat its 'object of study'.

Culture and Class: the Transition from Mob to Organised Labour

The nineteenth-century English working class developed its distinctive *class* organisations following the defeat of Chartism, but these were far from revolutionary; in general, the working class lacked the political organisation and leadership necessary for any effective challenge to bourgeois hegemony. Thus the major tradition in English fiction — bourgeois realism — either ignored or caricatured the industrial proletariat. Writing of the Victorian novel, George Orwell observes that 'if you look for the working class ... all you find is a hole ... the ordinary town proletariat, the people who make the wheels go round have always been ignored ...'. If they are noticed by writers, Orwell goes on, they are portrayed more or less as savages: 'Revolution is not a thing to be hoped for: it simply means the swamping of civilisation by the sub-human.' [4] Within the great tradition of the English novel, the emerging working class is either absent or depicted not as a *class* but as a *mob*: the eighteenth-century concept of an undisciplined, primitive, irrational and unstructured *mass* finds expression in such novels as Mrs Gaskell's *North and South* and *Mary Barton*, Dickens's *Barnaby Rudge* and *A Tale of Two Cities* and George Eliot's *Felix Holt* — fiction which postulates as the only hope of progress 'wise' middle-class leadership of the labour movement. The mainstream of nineteenth-century fiction denied the working class any real form of political or cultural independence; the working class is portrayed either in terms of a 'mob' or, as in Hoggart's *The Uses of Literacy*, largely passive, pragmatic and planless, incapable of generating democratic, political opposition to the ruling class. [5]

Orwell's general point, however, is not true of all forms of nineteenth-century fiction. Outside the major tradition, attempts were made to portray the working class as a *class* although, prior to the socialist revival of the 1880s, not a single realist novel was set *entirely* within a working-class environment. In the

'Chartist' novelists (Ernest Jones, Thomas Martin Wheeler), middle-class romance coexists with realistic detail of proletarian life within a fictional structure dominated by the literary conventions of the major tradition.[6] The same is true of the later, explicitly political fictions of such writers as Margaret Harkness and H. J. Bramsbury.[7] Engels's well-known comments on Margaret Harkness's novel *A City Girl* (1888) made this observation: a socialist novel, he wrote, achieved its purpose not through a direct political commitment, but by depicting the bourgeois world realistically, that is, 'by breaking down conventional illusions' and inducing doubt on 'the eternal character of the existing order, although the author does not offer any definite solution or . . . line up openly on any particular side'.[8] It was during the 1880s that working-class agitation revived through a series of violent strikes and lockouts and an unprecedented growth of trade unionism, especially among the unskilled workers (the 'New Unionism'). A Marxist political party, the Social Democratic Federation was formed in 1884 followed three years later by William Morris's Socialist League. The working-class movement was moving quickly to social and political independence although it was not until the turn of the century that the Independent Labour party was finally formed.

The 1880s was also the period of the great economic depression which had started in the 1870s and lasted until 1896, creating terrible hardship among the relatively new urban proletariat. All these tendencies combined to focus attention on the 'labour question' which in fiction found its expression in an increasing concern over the problem of social order. Two concepts, one old, the other new, characterised the fictional approach to working-class culture: the revival of the notion of 'mob' and the development of an image of proletarian life as an 'abyss'. In George Gissing's early novels, for example, working-class culture is portrayed in terms of a Darwinian struggle for existence, squalid, oppressive and totally dominating an apathetic mass. Yet, should it become organised and united into political parties and trade unions, the apathetic proletariat is transformed into an irrational and dangerous mass, the *mob*.[9] The other, new image also emphasises the squalid, monotonous and hopeless nature of working-class life and the latent threat of

violent revolution contained within but, as Peter Keating has
pointed out, 'the repeated use of the word "abyss" marks the
real change of attitude. It reflects a feeling of despair at worsen-
ing social conditions and at the inability of existing institutions
to deal with the problem; it reflects also a corresponding concern
with the growing militancy of the working-class movement that
was apparent in public demonstrations, socialist politics, and
trade union activity.[10] Perhaps the most striking presentation of
this new concept was Jack London's *The People of the Abyss*
(1903), a sober, factual study of the London poor,while in fiction
it was Arthur Morrison's novel *A Child of the Jago* (1896) and
his stories *Tales of Mean Streets* (1890) that gave the view of
proletarian culture as 'outcast' and 'alien' its fullest literary expression. Morrison's fiction is significant because it is set entirely
within a working-class milieu, with the working-class characters
neither sentimentalised nor romanticised but firmly and
realistically portrayed against a definite class background.
Nonetheless, Morrison accepted uncritically the dominant conventions of Victorian fiction: the workers in his 'abyss' are
beyond hope, their culture one of violence, criminality and un-
remitting squalor, an environment which crushes all individuality and negates all possibility of change from within.
Working-class culture is devitalised and oppressive.[11]

In the fiction of Gissing, Harkness and Morrison, there is
hardly any sense of those great and tumultuous events of the
1880s which were to have such decisive consequences for the
development of English capitalism and the labour movement.
The working class is portrayed as largely passive and irrational,
lacking any independent point of view or genuine culture. The
workers as a class simply do not exist. They are depicted exter-
nally to work and the factory system, while the relation of work,
trade unionism and politics is never articulated. The first major
attempt to portray the working class in terms of work and the
social relations arising from work was undoubtedly Robert
Tressell's novel *The Ragged Trousered Philanthropists*, a
'wonderful book' as Orwell commented which recorded 'the
facts of working-class life... things that were everyday experience but which simply had not been noticed before'[12] even
by those writers with the greatest sympathy for the working

class. Unlike the other novelists discussed above, Tressell was the first to explore the culture of working-class life *from within* and to adopt, on the basis of this understanding and as an organic part of this culture, a definite socialist standpoint.

Robert Tressell: the Working Classes as Prisoners of the System

Robert Tressell (1870–1911) wrote *The Ragged Trousered Philanthropists* between 1908 and 1910 while working full time as a painter in the south-coast town of Hastings.* In the novel Hastings becomes Mugsborough, a predominantly middle-class town with hardly any factories or modern industry; the working class is largely employed by the corporation or in shops, transport and domestic service; unemployment is high, poverty is widespread. In his biography of Tressell, F. C. Ball describes Hastings, and thus Mugsborough, at the turn of the century:

> Ragged, barefoot, rickety children walked the streets ... groups of down-at-heel and dejected unemployed haunted the street corners. People in the Ore district were used to the sight of a file of old women hobbling through the streets to collect their weekly bread ration at the workhouse. Average expectation of life was forty-four years.[14]

---

*Tressell, like Gissing and Morrison, was not working-class in origin but born into an Irish middle-class family; he was well-educated and could speak several languages. After a period in South Africa he settled in Hastings in 1902 choosing to work among the proletariat and not seek a middle-class post in the professions or as a teacher. His novel was thus written from the inside by a man who shared the experiences of working-class life because he identified with them and their struggle completely. Tressell was sympathetic towards the Marxist Social Democratic Federation but he seemed not to have joined the Painters' Union or made any real attempts to organise those workers he knew either politically or industrially. According to his daughter, when he completed the novel he became increasingly pessimistic and made plans to emigrate to Canada and 'make a fresh start, this time forgetting his ragged trousered philanthropists who would not listen to sense and for whom he had written the book'.[15] He died in Liverpool where he had gone to find work that would pay for his passage to Canada. He died anonymously: *The Ragged Trousered Philanthropists* was not published until 1914 and then only in a severely cut version which for many years was regarded as definitive. The full text was not published finally until 1955.

Tressell's fictionalised proletariat reflects this particular situation in that its members are largely painters and decorators and not the organised trade unionist workers of the big industrial cities; they have no interest in or much sympathy for socialism or the Labour party and passively 'put up' with exploitation, unemployment and poverty. The novel describes the working class as politically and socially disunited and, in the circumstances of chronic unemployment as man against man. There is little in Tressell's novel of those traditional elements of working-class culture — mutuality and solidarity. Consciousness is dominated totally by bourgeois ideology: Tressell's workers accept an inferior status, privations and deprivations without once questioning the nature of a capitalist society they see as morally right and as a natural social order. In his preface, Tressell describes the purpose of his novel in sociological terms as an attempt to present 'a faithful picture of working-class life . . . to describe the relations existing between the workmen and their employers, the attitudes and feelings of these two classes towards each other; the condition of the workers during the different seasons of the year; their circumstances when at work and when out of employment: their pleasures, their intellectual outlook, their religious and political opinions and ideals'. The great significance of *The Ragged Trousered Philanthropists* clearly lies in its vivid reconstruction of an entirely working-class milieu. The only middle-class character in the novel (apart from the capitalists and wily councillors) is Barrington, a reserved, articulate man who, while working as a painter, enjoys no real contact with his fellow-workers; his role is merely that of a spokesman for revolutionary socialism.

But the point of Tressell's novel is the workers' indifference to every form of socialism. As was argued in Chapter Two, the capitalist social formation consists of a multiplicity of structural levels between and within which there are uneven and contradictory developments. The capitalist mode of production embraces not simply big industrial and financial capital but a plurality of small industrial and financial enterprises which overlap and interpenetrate each other. Within a capitalist social formation, therefore, the division of labour and class structure are not homogeneous but variegated with the different levels developing at their own tempos; class structure, organisation and political consciousness always present a highly complex and contradictory character with the different levels of the working class linked in their specific historical developments with the prevailing mode of production. In the seaside town of Mugsborough, with its absence of an industrial infrastructure, the proletariat clearly has a far less developed sense of class solidarity and class consciousness than those urban workers such as engineers, dockers, miners and railwaymen whose work and work organisation place them at the forefront of capitalist development. It is ironic, therefore, that the first real novel of the working class is set among 'working-class Tories', workers who lack a history and tradition of class militancy and union organisation and whose work function lies within an industrial sector on the periphery of the capitalist mode of production. Of course, capitalist social relations and ideology characteristic of modern industry and factory organisation have penetrated the less developed economy of Mugsborough and it is in this sense that Tressell's workers are typical of the working class as a whole. Nonetheless, there is a contradiction between Tressell's portrait of a *totally apathetic* working class and his avowed intention to show the necessity for a socialism that will arise inevitably from the specific conditions of working-class life and capitalist social relations. For what *The Ragged Trousered Philanthropists* shows is that 'incorporation' of the working class which was discussed in the previous chapter; Tressell's workers simply have no 'alternative vision', no model of a future society, their ideas on society are merely those imposed by the dominant class and ideology. Customs, habit and tradition, those tenacious elements which Trotsky identified as inimical to socialism, create a conservative working class which yields active consent to its own unfreedom and exploitation.

The novel is structured around the Sisyphusian labours of its working-class hero, Owen, to educate his fellow workers out of their total acceptance of capitalist ideology and social organisation. Owen is portrayed as an ascetic and rather eccentric individual who has no interest in horse-racing, sport or the 'tittle-tattle' which are the main concerns of the other workers. As we shall see in discussing other 'proletarian novels', this separation of the working-class hero from his class is one of the basic elements in virtually all fictional reconstructions of working-class culture. Owen *understands*; the workers do not. Capitalist ideology is triumphant.

Yet in a way this is to be unfair to Tressell. When his fictional workers identify overpopulation, marriage and machinery as the causes of poverty and unemployment, when they reject the extension of education to the working class and the building of local libraries and parks, they reflect those basic assumptions of the dominant ideology shared by millions of workers in all kinds of industry. For example, they accept inequality as a fact of life which cannot be changed: 'There's always been rich and poor in the world, and there always will be.' Owen's socialist argument that the social world is not an external, dominating and natural force but historical and man-made and thus amenable to change is rejected again and again: 'There *must* be masters, and *someone* 'as to take charge of the work and do the thinkin'!' This is an argument as common then as it is today although, unlike Tressell's workers, the modern proletarian does not reject trade unionism and socialism out of hand. Nonetheless, he may share their keen sense of individualism and definition of society as a natural order: 'The majority desired nothing but to be allowed to work, and as for their children, why "what was good enough for themselves oughter be good enough for the kids".' [15] Bourgeois hegemony appears total; the capitalist social order is accepted as legitimate. Thus Owen reflects on the fact that capitalism is 'bound to fall to pieces because of its own rottenness', yet how difficult is the task of the socialist in face of those vast 'fortifications that surround the present system; the great barriers and ramparts of invincible ignorance, apathy and self-contempt, which will have to be broken down before the system of society of which they are the defences, can be swept away'! [16] Thus Orwell's argument that 'proletarian literature . . . is founded on the revolt against capitalism' [17] is confounded by Tressell's depiction of a working class that is neither in revolt nor angry. The novel's central message would seem to be the opposite of what a proletarian writer ought to assert: for it is Tressell's workers who are responsible for the maintenance of the capitalist system, they are the genuine philanthropists.

Throughout the novel, Owen continually returns to this pessimistic theme:

> All their lives they've been working like brutes and living in poverty. Although they have done more than their fair share of the work, they have never enjoyed anything like a fair share of the things thay have helped to produce. And yet, all their lives they have supported and defended the system that robbed them, and have resisted and ridiculed every proposal to alter it. It's wrong to feel sorry for such people; they deserve to suffer.[18]

Even after Owen has explained the mechanism of class exploitation ('The Money Trick') the workers insist on voting for the Tory party: 'Nothing delighted the childish minds of these poor people', Tressell writes, more than to read the extracts from the political speeches of Tories and Liberals that are 'full of cunning phrases intended to hoodwink the fools who had elected them'. When the local M.P., Sir Graball D'Encloseland, achieves government promotion, the hungry and unemployed Mugsborough workers 'boasted about it and assumed as much swagger in their gait as their broken boots permitted'. And finally, during the election rally, the workers, asked to wait some five hundred years before there is real social reform, enthusiastically endorse capitalist generosity: ' "Yes, Sir: we'll wait a thousand years if you like, Sir! ... I've .waited all my life, hoping and trusting for better conditions so a few more years won't make much difference to *me*" '.[19]

Tressell's workers, then, are those 'deferential' working-class Tory voters whom contemporary sociological research has identified as one of the most important supports for the maintenance of the capitalist social order in this century; in the most industrialised capitalist society in western Europe, a society containing a powerful trade union and labour movement, the Conservative party would have constituted a permanent opposition but for the security of that fifty per cent of its vote drawn from the working class.[20] The Mugsborough working class believes in natural hierarchies of class and status, passively it accepts the rigid notions that the country must be governed by 'those who know how', and that social change is always initiated from above. Human society is thus defined in reified terms:

> They accepted the present system in the same way as they accepted the alternating seasons. They knew that there was spring and summer and autumn and winter. As to how these different seasons came to be, or what caused them, they hadn't the remotest notion, and it is extremely doubtful whether the question had ever occurred to any of them. . . . From their infancy they had been trained to distrust their own intelligence, and to leave the management of the affairs of the world . . . to their betters . . . (accepting) as an established, incontrovertible fact that the existing state of affairs is immutable.[21]

Tressell's novel, then, is clearly built around a model of society similar to that employed by Horkheimer and other Frankfurt School theorists: a society of total management and manipulation, a system in which the contradictions are assimilated and negated by an overpowering, monolithic and fairly rigid capitalist ideology. It is not surprising, therefore, that Owen adopts a didactic and purely intellectual approach in his hopeless attempt to convert the workers to socialism and that he fails miserably to translate his personal beliefs into any form of meaningful action. The socialist pamphlets remain unread and irrelevant. Perhaps the point needs emphasising that, while the Mugsborough workers are representative of one element in the development of the modern working class, they cannot be taken as symptomatic of the historical evolution of the labour and trade union movement; the modern working class shares many of the illusions of these fictional workers but, even at the turn of the century, the working class as a whole was successfully building its own independent class institutions against the organised political and industrial opposition of the ruling class.

But for Tressell, working-class culture is hostile to the development of any form of socialist consciousness and praxis. In their depiction of working-class life, Morrison and Gissing had characterised the workers as victims of a dominating physical environment, of squalor, ignorance and poverty, but

Tressell goes beyond this limited concept of milieu to portray the dependence of the local environment on the capitalist system as a whole. It is the system of private property and exploitation which dominates these workers; the sheer monotony and boredom of working-class life is documented in great detail as with Morrison and Gissing (see especially the chapter ironically called 'The Financiers' which is taken up entirely with such apparently mundane, though important, details of working-class culture as the minutiae of the household budget). But Tressell is far more concerned to show how this is necessarily linked to the more abstract and general problems of class power and the distribution of wealth. The cultural life of the working class flows directly from the capitalist division of labour and, although Tressell never discusses the concept, from surplus value. *The Ragged Trousered Philanthropists* portrays the worker and his labour power as commodities and work as an alienated, devitalised and 'forced activity'. Work within the capitalist mode of production and its division of labour is neither an expression of an inner need nor a creative activity but simply a means whereby the individual survives within a hostile world. Time itself becomes an external and alien force that must be endured: when 'the workers arrived in the morning they wished it was breakfast-time. When they resumed work after breakfast they wished it was dinner-time. After dinner they wished it was one o'clock on Saturday. So they went on, day after day, year after year, wishing their time was over and, without realising it, really wishing that they were dead.' [22]

Although Tressell's portrait of working-class life is in terms of the necessary relation of work to capitalist exploitation and the resulting degeneration of work's creative potential in the interests of profit, the overriding impression is of a static and unchanging world in which there is no hope for radical social change. Working-class culture is dominated by capitalist ideology to the exclusion of any form of socialist alternative. Therefore, if *The Ragged Trousered Philanthropists* is to be defined as a proletarian novel, it is obviously not because of its depiction of a socialist or even potentially socialist working class but rather by virtue of its implication that a socialist consciousness has to be brought to the proletariat from outside by radical middle-class intellectuals (that is, the figure of Barrington). For Tressell, socialism in either its intellectual or its organisational expression does not arise organically from within the working class. The Mugsborough proletariat enjoys little sense of mutuality, class solidarity and class consciousness; its values are those of individualism and not collectivism.

The socialist standpoint within the novel, then, is opposed to Marx's injunction that the task of emancipating the workers was the task of the workers themselves. Without middle-class leadership there is no hope: the proletariat can achieve nothing of any political or social significance through its own efforts. Such thorough-going pessimism is thus mingled with a contempt for the working class. At the annual day-out ('The Beano'), Tressell gives vent to a total despair in his description of the exploited workers effusively endorsing their employer's enunciation of the virtues of class harmony and collaboration for the common good:

> The masters could not do without the men, and the men could not live without the masters. ('Hear, hear'.) It was a matter of division of labour: the men worked with their hands and the masters worked with their brains, and one was no use without the other. He hoped the good feeling which had hitherto existed between himself and his workmen would always continue, and he thanked them for the way in which they had responded to the toast of this health.[23]

The political message of Tressell's novel is thus clear: as Barrington puts it, it is not the rich who are responsible but 'the working classes themselves, who demand and vote for the continuance of the present system'.[24] It is hardly surprising, therefore, that Barrington (and presumably Tressell) offers a variety of state socialism whereby the gullible, 'childish' and passive workers are freed from class exploitation by action *from above*. The novel ends with an optimistic Barrington planning to open a local branch of the Social Democratic Federation with the help of money from his wealthy father. Such an élitist and utopian conclusion is thus bound up with Tressell's literary evocation of a working-class culture inimical to socialism, a culture lacking any real independence from the dominant class. The first significant novel about the working class is thus as pessimistic as those fictions which made no pretence to any form of political commitment or to a grasp of the dynamics of capitalist society. There is neither anger from within the working class at its deprivations nor any sense of revolutionary potential. *The Ragged Trousered Philanthropists* represents a conservative affirmation of the subordinate role played by the working class through a culture which is no more than the sum of habit, customs, superstition, ignorance and the compelling exigencies of everyday life.

Walter Greenwood and Grassic Gibbon: Reformism and Revolution

It has been argued above that Tressell's description of the English working class during the first years of the twentieth century as passive, individualistic and anti-socialist was atypical of the broader historical development of the labour movement. But of course the great majority of the urban working class did share many of these values and attitudes and uncritically accepted the legitimacy of capitalist society and the assumptions of bourgeois ideology. In his memoir of life in the Lancashire town of Salford from 1900 to 1920, Robert Roberts writes of the widespread 'apathy, docility, deference' of the 'ultra-patriotic mass' who 'remained intensely loyal to the nation and the system as a whole', looking 'upon social and economic inequality as the law of nature'. The urban slum, he suggests, was non-political for it could not be otherwise in a society in which nationally organised bourgeois political parties dominate over a weak, badly organised socialist movement.[25] But the historical and dynamic character of a social class, the complex and contradictory elements in its structure are eliminated when a *part* is taken for the *whole*. The Mugsborough workers, for example, represent one aspect of the working class as a historical phenomenon but not its totality.

A similarly one-sided interpretation of working-class life is evidenced in Orwell's *The Road to Wigan Pier* (1936). If Tressell emphasises the overpowering influence of bourgeois ideology on working-class consciousness, Orwell is more concerned with the workers' humane qualities of gregariousness, emotional warmth and solidarity:

> In a working-class home ... you breathe a warm, decent, deeply human atmosphere which is not so easy to find elsewhere. I should say that a manual worker, if he is in steady work and drawing good wages ... has a better chance of being happy than an 'educated' man. His home life seems to fall more naturally into a sane and comely shape.... Especially on winter evenings after tea, when the fire glows in the open range ... when Father, in shirt sleeves, sits in the rocking chair at one side of the fire reading the racing finals, and Mother sits on the other with her sewing, and the children are happy with a pennoth of mint humbugs ... it is a good place to be in, provided that you can be not only in it but sufficiently *of* it to be taken for granted.[26]

This excessively idealised vision of working-class culture has been much criticised for its failure to understand that close proximity breeds enmity as much as friendship and that working-class culture frequently revolves around a strict division of labour in the home in which the male role is dominant as well as a strict fidelity to conformist norms. Orwell and Hoggart are the polar opposites of Tressell in their romantic reduction of proletarian culture to a closed environmental structure – a variety of 'proletkult' that is peculiarly English.

Two novels published during that 1930s illustrate these two dominant trends in proletarian fiction, that is, the strictly political and the strictly cultural: Walter Greenwood's *Love on the Dole* (1933) and Lewis Grassic Gibbon's *A Scots Quair* (1932–4). Greenwood's novel covers the period from the mid-twenties to the formation of the second Labour government (1929–31) while Gibbon's trilogy portrays the years preceding the 1914–18 War to 1934. Both writers are concerned to depict the proletariat during a period of profound economic and social crisis when the ruling class was challenged by the growing power of the trade union and labour movement. Tressell's novel had been set at a time before the great expansion of the trade un-

ion movement and the emergence of the Labour party as a
national and political entity which finally formed the first
socialist administration in the minority government of 1924.
Roberts writes that after 1918 the working class was no longer
prepared to put up with massive inequalities yet the fact remains
that the inter-war years witnessed massive long-term unemployment, widespread poverty and a crushing defeat for the labour
movement in the General Strike of 1926. How does *Love on the
Dole* come to terms with working-class culture in the face of
these momentous events?

Unlike Tressell, Greenwood is not concerned with showing
the necessity for socialism and there is no clear political commitment other than a sense of outrage at the tragic social consequences of mass unemployment. Indeed, on one level, *Love on
the Dole* is a reversal to mythologising working-class life
through a gallery of types such as the disreputable villain (Ned
Narkey, Sam Grundy), the beautiful heroine, Sally Hardcastle,
whom Greenwood describes as 'a gorgeous creature', and the
ascetic, working-class hero, Larry Meath. At times the novel
reads like a caricature rather than a realistic presentation of
working-class life and the tone degenerates to the level of cheap
magazine fiction as in this description of sexual attraction:

> He could feel the quick sharp gusts of her breathing; her lips
> were almost touching his: his head dropped involuntarily, ef-
> fortlessly and a wild, dizzying ebullience swept through him.
> His arm stole about her in a close embrace.[27]

For Greenwood, working-class culture is defined not in terms of
the social relations of production and the exploitation of labour
through the work situation (work is simply in the background)
or of praxis but quite simply of Trotsky's concept of those
'tenacious' habits and customs which dominate the life situation
of the Salford proletariat: the pub, football, betting and
newspaper competitions (today it would be television quiz
programmes) combine with a puritanical sexual code and a
widespread sense of 'respectability' and hence status in the community to create a working class which conforms completely to
bourgeois society and bourgeois values. The notion of 'respec-

tability' is perhaps the major key for understanding the novel's structure and its depiction of working-class culture. At the end of the nineteenth century, Engels wrote of a deep sense of respectability 'bred into the bones of the workers' and his description of 'the social division of society into innumerable gradations, each recognised without question, each with its own pride but also its inborn respect for its "betters" and "superiors" ...' aptly characterised Tressell's fictional workers, but only at the level of political consciousness. Greenwood's working class is respectable in a rather different sense: the essence of respectability lies in the notion of decency − it is considered 'indecent', for example, to be in debt ('Fair play, *that's* my motto. Owe nowt t'nobody an' stare everybody in face'), to engage in premarital sex, to be pregnant before marriage or to steal from the local shops.[28] This concept of respectability is meant to divide one section of the working class from the other and it accounts for status divisions within the class itself and the local community. Yet the vast majority of working-class people would always define themselves as respectable even though their life styles might not conform with the dominant norms. Respectability can also include trade union and political activity, but for Greenwood, the workers as a mass accept an individualistic rather than a collectivist notion which, as will be argued below, is indicative of a middle-class view of 'proletarian culture'.

Greenwood's elimination of the political determinations of class culture is linked closely to the essentially static and ahistorical framework of the novel: while the novel spans the tumultuous years from 1924 to 1931, the really significant events such as the General Strike and the forming of the second Labour government appear to have no meaning or relevance to the lives of the fictional workers. The result is a presentation of working-class life that is both fixed and unchanging (see especially the second chapter and the last section of the final chapter) in which the characters lack the most rudimentary form of class consciousness. Trade unionism, for example, plays no significant role within the novel and working-class life is described apart from its most characteristic institution. Within the working-class community, it is not the values of solidarity and mutuality but egoism and individualism and the desire to 'get on' or 'get out' which constitute the basic structure of the culture. The novel's message seems to suggest the futility of struggling to improve the situation from within: when the workers, having heard that their unemployment benefits are to be cut, march on the Labour Exchange, they quickly turn into an irrational mob at the mercy of outside agitators.[29] There seems no way in which the working class can organise itself as a class: resistance is futile and the only possible attitude is one of stoic endurance against appalling deprivations.

Love on the Dole is not a proletarian novel. Its portrait of working-class culture is partial and ideological even to the extent of its language. Greenwood allows the workers to speak their own language but frequently intrudes an authorial presence to explain (to the middle-class reader, presumably) what they mean: ' "Ar owld man (father)..." ' and ' "Ah've come out bout (without) me baskit..." '.[30] More seriously, the socialist hero, Larry, is presented, like Owen in *The Ragged Trousered Philanthropists*, as the embodiment of conventional morality and English middle-class values. He has no dialect; he does not swear, drink, gamble or brawl. When he attempts to explain the basics of socialist economics to his fellow workers, his complete failure to communicate is exaggerated by the use of perfect English. Larry is excessively polite, he raises his hat to Sally and he enjoys classical music. These characteristics separate him from the workers as an eccentric and an atypical representative of their interests. He does not participate in working-class activities; he is the ascetic socialist who preaches reason at the height of the riot only to be ignored by the irrational mob. He is impotent in every way, his set pieces on socialist theory having no effect on an indifferent proletariat.

Passivity, therefore, is the major structure in *Love on the Dole*. Harry Hardcastle, Sally's younger brother, becomes the innocent victim of a situation that cannot be changed; human activity can have no effect and the individual must either adapt or hope for a lucky break. The novel ends with Harry in work simply because Sally has accepted Sam Grundy as her lover while his friend Jack remains among the army of the unemployed:

No influential person to pull strings on his behalf; no wages for him tonight; no planning for the morrow. He was an anonymous unit of an army of three millions for whom there was no tomorrow.[31]

Respectability is finally saved because Harry has money and therefore hope: the role of money in the novel is double-edged for, while Greenwood rightly stresses its dominant function in working-class life (in Mr Hardcastle's phrase, 'Blimey, man, d'y' think blasted money grows on trees.') with its practical human consequences (Harry can't afford to get married), money is seen as sufficient in itself bringing status and creating the basis of social cohesion. The novel portrays the working classes as reasonably affluent before the slump of 1931 because they earned good wages. The implication is obvious: when the slump is over money will once again be plentiful and the working classes contented with their lot.

In sharp contrast, Grassic Gibbon's novel is overtly political and historical as it strives to depict the development of the Scottish working class from its roots in farming and agriculture at the turn of the century to its necessary (and inevitable) emergence as an organised urban mass deeply involved in class struggle. *Love on the Dole* is not concerned with the class struggle and fails to make any artistic link between modern capitalist industry and the social relations and values of working-class culture. *A Scots Quair*, however, differs from the works of both Tressell and Greenwood in that this relationship is rendered ideologically since the novel does not place the proletariat at its centre; its milieu is agricultural and middle-class. Its status as a proletarian novel hinges entirely on its political commitment to socialism and not on any organic presentation of working-class life. Thus the first volume, *Sunset Song*, describes the harsh life of tenant farming and the rise of capitalist agriculture; *Cloud Howe* and *Grey Granite* take the novel's heroine, Chris Guthrie, from her marriage to a clergyman through to the final scenes of her son Ewan's conscious political choice and rejection of middle-class values. The strength of *A Scots Quair* lies in its grasp of the historical background: in *Sunset Song*, the life of each character is shaped

decisively by historical events taking place outside the small farming community and culminating in the First World War. But
in the subsequent volumes, this organic relation of individual to
history is much weaker and great social events such as the
General Strike and the Hunger Marches of the early 1930s
merely provide the narrative with a historical dimension and a
rationale for Ewan's inevitable decision to join the Communist
party. Raymond William's assertion that Grassic Gibbon's
novel 'embodies the active labour movement of the thirties' [32] is
misleading for the whole weight of the last two volumes lies in
their uncritical affirmation of the Communist party's
programme and ideology as representative of the whole labour
movement. Nothing could be further from the truth: the Stalinist
and bureaucratic Communist party held no decisive sway over
the British working class nor could it have done so given its
slavish adherence to the Moscow leadership. There was never
any organic relation between the party and the working class:
the point that is made in the novel about the failure of the
General Strike and the fiasco of the second Labour government
is that there was a historic necessity for a new political
leadership of the left outside the Labour party. In the context of
the 1930s, such sectarian solutions were merely utopian.

Yet, for all its support for Communism, Grassic Gibbon's
novel is not really about the proletariat: in *Sunset Song* the lives
of the poor tenant farmers and peasants are invested with great
richness and individuality that are far from the monotonous and
squalid experiences of Morrison's and Gissing's urban workers;
their work, too, is actively and organically set within the community and with their deep sense of independence goes a pride
with themselves and their work. This is shown in the episode
when John Guthrie is deciding on his new farm:

But the rent was awful high and he saw that nearly all the dis-
trict was land of the large-like farm, he'd be squeezed to death
and he'd stand no chance. It was fine land though, that nearly
shook him, fine it looked and your hands they itched to be at
it; but the agent called him *Guthrie*, and he fired up at the
agent: *Who the hell are you Guthrie-ing? Mister Guthrie to
you*. And the agent looked at him and turned right white to

the gills, and then gave a bit of a laugh and said *Ah well, Mr. Guthrie I'm afraid you won't suit us*. And John Guthrie said *It's your place that doesn't suit me ... you wee, dowp-licking clerk*. Poor he might be but the creature wasn't yet clecked that might put on its airs with him, John Guthrie.[33]

Yet in the final volume, *Grey Granite*, the industrial town and its factory proletariat have become mere shadows – the necessary background to Ewan's gradual disillusionment with the Labour left and his acceptance of Communism. He consciously joins the workers by taking up an apprenticeship rather than a university course, a tactic which doubtless has its roots in the anti-intellectualism of Stalinist politics. At first, he despises and remains apart from his fellow workers, but unlike the other intellectual ascetic heroes of Tressell's and Greenwood's novels, Grassic Gibbon's hero has the enormous advantage that the distance between himself and the masses is necessarily bridged by the knowledge that the working class and the Communist party embody the sole hope for social change. Revolution is inevitable: 'A hell of a thing to be History! – not a student, a historian, a tinkling reformer, but LIVING HISTORY ONESELF, being it, making it, eyes for the eyeless, hands for the maimed!'. The trilogy closes with Ewan's total assimilation into the Stalinist politics of the thirties:

> '*I'm a Communist*. And fell to his whistling again, but soberly. And when he next spoke there was steel in his voice, the steel of a cold, unimpassioned hate: *I could tell long ago that Seldon would rat; you can tell a rat easily among revolutionists – yeasty sentiment and blah about Justice. They think they're in politics or a parlour game*.[34]

Ideology has taken over the fictional structure completely: *A Scots Quair* closes with the 'iron man' about to lead the revolutionary working class away from the Labour party into a combative Communist movement. Thus the relationship of party and class is hierarchical and élitist: the Party understands history and the proletariat must be yoked into its inevitable role. Working-class culture is therefore identified with the 'vanguard' party and it has no real independence from it. The workers are the agents of history: Tressell's workers may be passive and deferential but they are genuine human beings embedded in a distinctively working-class milieu; Grassic Gibbon's proletariat is a lifeless mouthpiece for Stalinist orthodoxy. Revolution is to be imposed from above and is not bound organically with the real life experiences of the working class and its dominant institutions. Both Tressell and Grassic Gibbon share this conception, and it is this more than anything else which illustrates the weakness of the so-called proletarian novel.

The Welfare State, Egalitarian Ideology and Working-Class Culture: Braine, Sillitoe and Hines

During the 1930s the working class endured defeat in both Britain and Europe. The Conservative governments of Baldwin and Chamberlain and the triumph of fascism in Italy and Germany were grounded in the failure of European socialism and communism to provide decisive leadership and policy. In such a context, literary affirmations of a revolutionary proletariat were clearly absurd; with the coming of the Popular Front in the mid-thirties (an alliance between the 'progessive' bourgeoisie and the defeated Communist parties and the socialists) the concept of proletarian culture and fiction in all its forms virtually disappeared. It was not until after 1945 that the working class reappeared in modern fiction and then in a very different form from the workers depicted by Tressell, Greenwood and Grassic Gibbon. The first majority Labour government came to power in 1945 to carry through a series of far-reaching reforms in industry, education, health and employment thus laying the foundations of the modern welfare state. The historic significance of the Labour administration lies not so much in its modest (and abortive) attempts to redistribute income or challenge the balance of power in society as in the fact that for the first time since the General Strike the labour movement with its organisations could again gather confidence in its sense of independence and ability to fight for its members. Trade union membership increased while its role in government became more and more critical. Without the active support of the unions, capitalist domination would have become exceedingly problematical; the major industrial institution of the working class was now at the centre of government acting for its members within the context of a triumphant political reformism. The positive content of this reformism was of course the welfare state which had the effect of generating a widespread sense of egalitarianism; the post-war period was characterised by the view that the old ways (massive unemployment, poverty and inequality) belonged to the past and that a new, more humane society was in the making. These developments, together with the decline in influence ·of the Communist party and the failure of other left-wing groups to build any meaningful relation with the working class, constituted the basis of a radically different literary approach to working-class culture. Two novels especially embody this transition from the Tressell/Grassic Gibbon/Greenwood model of a largely inert proletariat to the new, more aggressive and independent view of the working class, even though neither fiction directly portrays working-class nor exemplifies a socialist tendency.

Philip Larkin's *Jill* (1946) and John Braine's *Room at the Top* (1957) portray the attempted assimilation of the intelligent grammar-school working-class boy into middle-class culture. Larkin's anti-hero, John Kemp, consciously rejects his respectable working class parents in favour of a philistine bourgeois culture and an ascribed status he can never attain. A 'scholarship boy' in the same mould as that described in Hoggart's *The Uses of Literacy*, John Kemp has not the necessary inner strength to resist the blandishments of his bourgeois student companions in wartime Oxford; he has neither a meaningful link with his class background nor any consciousness of class. Larkin's novel, therefore, remains firmly within the static tradition of the pre-war proletarian writers in that the class and status system is uncritically accepted by its working-class anti-hero as something which is *there*. *Room at the Top* also depicts a fixed class structure but, whereas Larkin's John Kemp retreats to a closed fantasy world in which he and a non-existent sister, Jill, possess those bourgeois cultural attributes he yearns for in real life, Braine's hero, Joe Lampton, aggressively and confidently pursues the ambition of high social

status, motivated by an overpowering sense of *envy*. Joe Lampton is the genuine post-war working-class hero whose values and
goals are no longer restricted by a passive acceptance of the
class system but have been shaped by the apparent contradiction between the egalitarian ideals of the welfare state and a
society built on inequality and subordination. Joe Lampton
refuses to accept his 'natural' place in the social hierarchy, 'the
smell of security and servitude'.[35] Braine's hero enjoys a greater
sense of class consciousness than any worker in Tressell,
Grassic Gibbon or Greenwood's novels. This is reflected in such
apparently trivial details as wearing a shirt for the second day
running ('I had the working-class mentality; anything was good
enough for work.'), his feeling that his teeth are working-class,
not being as white as middle-class teeth, the unease with 'posh
restaurants' and his constant grading of individuals exclusively
in terms of income. And during confinement in a German
prisoner-of-war camp he chooses study rather than escape:
'Those three years were the only chance I'd get to be qualified.
Let those rich bastards who have all the fun be heroes. Let them
pay for their privileges. If you want it straight from the shoulder
I'll tell you: I was bloody well pleased when I was captured.' [36]
To be sure, Joe Lampton's values are those of individualism and
egoism; he rejects the masses as 'zombies' and is opposed to all
forms of collectivism. His envy fuels his ambitions: 'The rich
were my enemies, I felt: they were watching me for the first false
move.'[37]   It is this awareness, combined with Lampton's
aggressive sense of outrage and anger, which links *Room at the
Top* with the first real proletarian novel, Alan Sillitoe's *Saturday
Night and Sunday Morning* (1958).

Sillitoe's hero is a skilled factory worker, Arthur Seaton, and
the novel chronicles his family, work, leisure and general outlook without any sentimentality or recourse to middle-class
values and characters. The milieu and the people are totally
working-class. This fact alone gives the novel its great
significance for here is the authentic working class of modern
capitalism. Arthur Seaton, like Joe Lampton, has a deep sense of
outrage against society but, unlike Braine's hero, he strives to
assert his integrity as a human being within a working-class
situation he accepts as his own and in full knowledge of the

system which oppresses him. There is no envy or desire to 'get on' and 'get out', only a deep commitment to the values of a working-class culture which acts as a fortification against the class enemy, *them*. Unlike Greenwood's workers, Arthur Seaton does not passively adapt to the situation but actively seeks to 'get at *them*' – the collective forces of social order and oppression. In his fine short story, *The Loneliness of the Long Distance Runner*, Sillitoe describes how his borstal boy runner deliberately loses an important cross-country race he is expected to win to affirm his independence from *them*. As with Arthur Seaton, it is the quality of cunning which counts: 'I'm telling you straight: they're cunning, and I'm cunning. If only "them" and "us" had the same idea we'd get on like a house on fire, but they don't see eye to eye with us and we don't see eye to eye with them, so that's how it stands and how it will always stand.' [38] Faced with a hostile world, Sillitoe's heroes retain their individuality not through 'knuckling under' as is the case with some of Arthur's fellow workers but by a conscious rejection of those rules and values which belong to the world of *them*. In both the short story and the novel, Sillitoe's social vision is individualistic and broadly anarchical with a total repudiation of the political system, trade unions and all forms of private and public authority.

Unlike Grassic Gibbon, Sillitoe does not reduce his working class to a mere puppet of history but he does portray the workers as a mass which has become integrated into capitalist society largely through the pervasive influence of the mass media – television in particular. Working-class culture is thus depicted as a conservative force binding the working class to the capitalist social order and incapable of sustaining any real opposition to the existing system except on the purely individual level. Arthur Seaton as an individual may be 'rough' rather than 'respectable' in his pursuit of married women and his pointless acts of violence and hostility to law and order. But the close-knit, respectable working-class family finally claims him as its own at the close of the novel, the power of conformity to norms being greater than an idiosyncratic anarchism.

Saturday Night and Sunday Morning is thus the major working-class novel that the other fiction we have been discussing is not. Sillitoe restores the speech of working-class people to its proper dignity as concrete, direct and essentially debunking; he is also aware of the clichés which dominate the everyday talk. He portrays a self-contained culture built around the pub, gambling, fishing and a dense web of family relations. It is a culture which has both great vitality and a limited potential, for it is a culture in which the proletariat remains a subordinate class seemingly unable to develop beyond the negative aggression of Arthur Seaton. *Saturday Night and Sunday Morning* is thus profoundly conservative, neither a revolutionary nor a socialist novel. For how could it be otherwise? Sillitoe's working class is not the abject, defeated proletariat of the 1920s and 1930s but a class in full employment, earning relatively high wages and defended by a strong trade union movement. It is not a working class which is preparing to challenge the cultural and social domination of the ruling class but one which accepts the legitimacy of reform within the political framework of Social Democracy. This is not to argue that the workers are a docile and passive mass, only that there is no other alternative to political reformism and economism and that the class struggle necessarily takes place within those working-class institutions and therefore takes on a peaceful but dogged and resilient character. The proletarian novel, almost by definition, must fail to understand this aspect of the modern class struggle and it is against the apparent docility of his fellow workers that Arthur Seaton's rebellious and violent acts have their meaning. *Saturday Night and Sunday Morning* offers no panaceas – neither Greenwood's 'getting on' nor Tressell's and Grassic Gibbon's substitutive political élitism but a quiet recognition that the proletariat is a mass and yet a recognisable class. With the continued domination of bourgeois ideology, social democracy and reformism combined with the weakness of Marxism and left politics in Britain, this is a portrait both historically accurate and artistically complete.

Much the same is true of another proletarian fiction, Barry Hines's *A Kestrel for a Knave* (1968) which, like Sillitoe's novel, is set entirely within a working-class culture; unlike *Saturday Night and Sunday Morning*, however, Hines is describing the 'rough' rather than the 'respectable' working class in an environment of harsh deprivation. Billy Casper comes from a broken home, his mother neglects him in favour of the local pub and men, he becomes a delinquent stealing from shops and doorways and an incorrigible liar. His family life is dominated by betting, boozing and emotional starvation. Social and cultural deprivations are total: Billy does badly at school and identifies it as a hostile, middle-class institution. His attitude towards authority is superficially similar to Arthur Seaton's but more muted and pathetic: Billy Casper is the typical reject of the welfare state and its educational system; defined and labelled as a failure by his teachers, he seems passively to accept his role. Yet he doesn't. For one thing, Billy is fully aware of the teachers' negative definition of him and the others:

> They're not bothered about us, just because we're in 4C, you can tell, they talk to us like muck. They're allus callin' us idiots, an' numbskulls, an' cretins, an' looking at their watches to see how long it is to t'end of t'lesson. They're fed up wi' us. We're fed up wi' them . . . .[39]

Like Arthur Seaton, Billy Casper is not an object but a person, an individual who is not simply getting back at *them* but actively pursuing a consuming interest in falconry. He captures a kestrel, which he calls Kes, and builds it a home in his garden and by absorbing himself in a stolen book becomes something of an expert on falconry. In one scene, Billy's teacher, on discovering his interest, becomes the pupil and Billy, the teacher. Thus, while the social vision within the novel is bleak and negative, Billy is not shown as a member of an anonymous mass, he is not 'just fodder for the mass media' as one teacher unkindly describes his class in school.

For Billy, the captured hawk has an independence and a pride which are missing from his own life-situation. The hawk is not kept as a pet for, although Billy has trained it, 'It's fierce, an' it's wild, an' it's not bothered about anybody, not even about me right. And that's why it's great.'[40] When the hawk is killed by Billy's older brother in a fit of anger, the sense of deprivation, hopelessness and resignation is complete: working-class culture is here depicted as a wasteland lacking that vitality which characterises *Saturday Night and Sunday Morning*. Yet Hines's novel is authentically working-class and a grimly contemporary and realistic picture of class inequality.

The Myth of the Proletarian Novel

From Tressell to Sillitoe and Hines, the dominant tendency in the literary depiction of the working class has been in terms of 'incorporation', mass society and passivity. From these fictions, a picture emerges of a proletariat which uncritically accepts bourgeois institutions and ideology; the workers have no pretensions to hegemony, no distinctive culture other than those values associated with the family and kin and the traditions and habits of a local community. At the level of ideology there is only that of the dominant class. The argument, therefore, of a 'common culture' which pervades all strata of society and is particularly exemplified in the art and literature of a culture, finds no expression in these writers except in Walter Greenwood's middle-class view of the working class.

As we have argued in Chapter Two, the concept of culture is both political and historical. It would seem that an authentic working-class fiction such as *Saturday Night and Sunday Morning* necessarily eliminates these specific determinations and defines culture not in terms of praxis but statically. Here is the great weakness of the proletarian novel: it divests the notion of class of its political and historical structures. Its great strength, however, lies in its grasp of the individual as an individual and its refusal to dissolve him into a mere object of history or the dupe of a mass society.

Chapter 4

Ideology and Mass Communications – the Problem of Legitimacy

The Capitalist State and Ideological Domination

As we have argued in previous chapters, underpinning the Marxist theories of the Frankfurt School (Marcuse, Horkheimer and Adorno) is a model of modern capitalist society as a mass society. Although there are differences of emphasis between these theorists, they all agree that, with the development of the capitalist mode of production, the civil institutions grow progressively weaker as the role of the state becomes more and more dominant in economic management and social and cultural organisation. In these circumstances the question of social integration devolves on the state and the notion of legitimacy itself becomes increasingly problematical. Marx's revolutionary class is now integrated from above by the 'culture industry' – the mass media of television, radio, newspapers and magazines. The dominant ideology is thus imposed on a passive, pliant mass: 'the result of a permanent and pervasive *effort*, conducted through a multitude of agencies, and deliberately intended ... to dissuade members of the subordinate classes, if not from holding, at least from voicing unorthodox views'. This argument of Ralph Miliband crudely echoes the pessimistic theories of the Frankfurt School and the two chapters of his book, *The State in Capitalist Society*, devoted to the problem of legitimacy constitute a sustained attempt to show that social integration is the direct result of 'a process of massive indoctrination'.[1] For Miliband, the state is now 'one of the main architects of the conservative consensus' whose ideological domination is supported by the institutions of civil society such as the mass media. These institutions function as 'agencies for the dissemination of ideas and values which affirm rather than challenge existing patterns of power and privilege ... weapons in the arsenal of class domination'. Miliband concludes:

> The mass media cannot ensure complete conservative attunement; nothing can. But they can and do contribute to the fostering of a climate of conformity, not by the total suppression of dissent, but by the presentation of views which fall outside the consensus as curious heresies. ...[2]

Social order is thus augmented by the ideological domination of a ruling class which effectively controls and in many cases owns the mass media: Miliband's model of society is implicitly totalitarian and comes remarkably close to a 'conspiracy theory'.

Strikingly similar to these formulations is Louis Althusser's theoretical study 'Ideology and Ideological State Apparatuses' (1969), which argues that the maintenance of capitalism hinges on its ability to reproduce 'submission to the rules of the established order, i. e. ... submission to the ruling ideology for the workers and ... to manipulate the ruling ideology correctly for the agents of exploitation and repression ...'. Like Miliband, Althusser accepts that the modern state plays a major role in achieving social integration and he makes the distinction between state institutions whose function is to maintain domination through potential force (the 'Repressive State Apparatus' such as the army and the police) and those other institutions which underpin bourgeois authority by the dissemination of ideology (the 'Ideological State Apparatus'). Althusser's main point is the 'plurality' of the Ideological State Apparatuses embracing such diverse institutions as education, law, religion, trade unions and the mass media. The classic distinction between private and public institutions and realms has disappeared: the state integrates the different social strata from above through 'direct domination' and force when necessary but more usually through 'indirect, ideological domination'.[3]

Both these arguments thus assert a theory of social integration and order through cultural institutions. It is important to emphasise that these Marxist interpretations stress that social integration flows from above – a forced and self-conscious process of class legitimation. It might be noted that other non-Marxist writers have accorded equal powers to the mass media although, in general, they tend to minimise the notion of integration from above:

> By expressing, dramatising, and repeating cultural patterns, both the traditional and the newly emerging, the media reinforce tradition and at the same time explain new roles. Members of the society thus remain integrated within the sociocultural structure. As a form of adult socialisation, the media are seen as guarantors that a body of common ultimate values remains visible as a continuing source of consensus, despite the inroads of change.[4]

The phrase, 'common ultimate values', suggests ideology: the question is the exact relation between the mass media, ideological processes and integration. Miliband and Althusser follow the Frankfurt School in identifying ideology with 'false consciousness' and the role of cultural institutions as the conveyor belts of class ideology. This chapter will explore the problems involved in such theories and especially the view that the mass media constitute a major mode of social integration and legitimation.

Legitimation and the Concept of Public Sphere

The rise of the masses coincides with industrialisation, political democracy, universal suffrage and class society. The term masses, however, is not identical with mass society; nineteenth-century capitalism brought into social and political prominence the urban, factory proletariat while the division of labour created the foundations for widespread skills and mass employment. Factory organisation generates class identification and class consciousness; class institutions and political awareness are thus bound up with the emergence of the proletariat as a *mass*. This development generates the first major crisis of bourgeois legitimacy.

In *The German Ideology*, Marx and Engels discussing the growth of capitalist society argued that the bourgeoisie, unlike previous dominant classes, would be forced to legitimise its authority not by appealing to a static traditionalism but through the more prosaic, secular and dynamic notion of ideology. To be sure, legitimacy grounded in tradition is ideological but, unlike pre-capitalist ruling classes, the bourgeoisie must rationalise its ideology and ground it firmly within the material and historical life of the society and in this way make its appeal to the class it must dominate. The major ideas of each epoch, wrote Marx and Engels, are those of the ruling class, for the class which controls 'the means of material production' will necessarily control 'the means of mental production'.[5] The capitalist division of labour continually refines this distinction between material labour and intellectual labour and with the evolution of modern civil society and the growth of the mass media of newspaper publishing, magazines and pulp fiction, mass political parties and educational institutions, the role of the intellectual becomes increasingly significant in the genesis and transmission of bourgeois ideology. Gramsci called such intellectuals 'experts in legitimation' whose function was to provide the basis of bourgeois authority in reason, humanity and progress. Of all dominant classes in history, the bourgeoisie is the only one which strengthens civil society and strives to augment its rule not by force but through consent and hegemony.[6] This concept of hegemony is based on Gramsci's distinction between private and public institutions, the former type (the family, church, trade unions and political parties) constituting the locus of class ideology and the transmission of bourgeois ʾ lues, aspirations and norms. Of course, in the complex structure of modern capitalist society, rigid demarcations cannot be made between these two types of institution, but Gramsci's main point was that the essence of bourgeois domination lay in its hegemonic authority over the realm of the private.

However, as we have seen, the tendency among contemporary Marxists is to reject the value of Gramsci's theoretical model of society and argue for a fusion of political and civil society. The Frankfurt School theorists have been particularly influential in this respect: their theory of mass society and the 'culture industry' is, in effect, a total rejection of the concept of hegemony; the modern state dominates civil society and the autonomous individual is crushed by the weight of a massive administrative apparatus. For these writers, the concept of 'public sphere' is their counterpart for Gramsci's 'hegemony', a concept developed by the European bourgeoisie in the battle against feudal ideology and absolutism: the public sphere was intended to mediate between the state and society and create a balance of forces in which capitalist enterprise could flourish. The classic expression, of the 'public sphere' concept was nineteenth-century liberal capitalism with its guarantee of the right of represen tation, freedom of speech and assembly and the efficacy of public opinion:

> *The bourgeois public sphere* (can) be understood as the sphere of private individuals assembled into a public body, which almost immediately laid claim to the officially regulated 'intellectual newspapers' for use against the public authority itself. In those newspapers, and in moralistic and critical journals, they debated that public authority on the general rules of social intercourse in their fundamentally privatised yet publically relevant sphere of labour and commodity exchange.[7]

For the Frankfurt School, the public sphere withers as the self-regulating liberal capitalism of the nineteenth century gives way to the regulated, planned and totally administered 'organised capitalism' of the twentieth century.

The Frankfurt School's theorising of the bourgeois notion of public sphere and Gramsci's theory of hegemony can be seen as two related though distinct solutions to the question of legitimacy in societies characterised by class conflict and the institutions of mass democracy. The rise of the working class during the nineteenth century posed the first threat to bourgeois legitimacy, a crisis in class domination which was partly solved by the absence of working-class political organisation and the failure of socialist ideas to penetrate large sections of the urban proletariat. Once established, however, bourgeois hegemony became the effective means for 'controlling' the development of working-class political organisation and their economic and social institutions. The late development of an independent English working-class party attests to the authority of bourgeois hegemony over the subordinate class. The socialising function of educational institutions, the embryonic mass media and the work discipline imposed by the capitalist division of labour thus supported rather than combatted bourgeois ideology. The working class was integrated into nineteenth-century capitalism precisely because it accepted the necessity for conducting the class struggle within the existing institutional framework: reformism and economism were thus the social correlates of political legitimacy.

But legitimacy is not a static process. As Marx noted, bourgeois society creates both the foundations for capitalist development and the institutions which must oppose and finally destroy it. Capitalism as an economic order generates not only the political and social institutions which facilitate the domination of the bourgeois class but also those socialist parties and working-class organisations which pose the major threat to bourgeois hegemony. Modern capitalism is a social order which solves its economic crises through the direct involvement of trade unions and working-class political parties in the management of government thus shifting the bases of legitimacy from a secure to a fragile foundation: the ruling class secures its domination through the consent of the dominated class, a process mediated by working-class institutions. The role of the mass media in the maintenance of bourgeois hegemony thus becomes critical.

Ideology and False Consciousness: Althusser and Poulantzas

In the writings of many contemporary Marxists, capitalist domination flows immediately from the propagation of bourgeois ideology by the mass media. In Chapter Three it was noted that the major trend in proletarian fiction was to buttress these pessimistic conclusions and portray modern society as a mass society in which the working class (apart from the exceptional individual) had become indistinguishable from the passive 'proles' of Orwell's *Nineteen Eighty-Four:* indeed, Orwell's model of society as totally managed and manipulated by the ruling élite is remarkably close to the depiction of contemporary capitalism as regulated by the state and the cultural apparatuses. What is being asserted, therefore, is a totalitarian model of society in which the dominant ideology works to corrupt the consciousness of the working class. In short, the working class has come to acquire a 'false consciousness', aspiring to the 'false needs' of a consumer-oriented capitalism which consequently deflects it from the historic mission of developing a revolutionary class consciousness, socialist organisation and praxis.

Yet the relation of ideology to the mass media is far more problematic than these mechanical formulations suggest. For Adorno, Miliband and Althusser, ideology works one way, that is, from above, seeping into working-class organisations and consciousness as an alien, conservative force. The concept of ideology at the heart of these arguments is one which relates directly to the notion of mass society and the resultant absence of hegemony (or the disintegration of the public sphere). If a model of capitalism as mass society is used, ideology must always be defined as 'false consciousness'.

The concept of 'false consciousness', however, is more complex than these usages suggest: for if defined in this way it constitutes an idealist rather than scientific understanding of the social world. This conflation of ideology and false consciousness is one of Engels's more confusing contributions to Marxism: 'Ideology is a process accomplished by the so-called thinker consciously indeed but with a false consciousness. The real motives impelling him remain unknown ... otherwise it would

not be an ideological process at all.'[8] Marx rarely uses ideology
in this sense of pure illusion as his analysis of eighteenth-century
political economy (in his monumental *Theories of Surplus
Value*) makes clear. On the basis of Engels's argument, it would
seem that only Marxism itself can escape the blight of false consciousness. Yet, while it is quite valid to postulate a dependent
relation between ideas and social structure, it does not necessarily follow that all ideas are errors, distortions and illusions.[9] This
is Lenin's understanding when he uses the term 'socialist
ideology':

> Socialism, in so far as it is the ideology of struggle of the
> proletarian class, undergoes the general conditions of birth,
> development and consolidation of an ideology, that is to say,
> it is founded on all the material of human knowledge, it
> presupposes a high level of science ... (and) scientific
> work ....[10]

Lenin's concept of ideology is thus opposed to those who define
it as a form of deception and illusion. For the corollary of false
consciousness is true consciousness and if all ideology is illusion
and error then it becomes impossible to grasp the sociological
foundations of ideological thought: it is through ideology,
whether this takes the form of common sense or the elaboration
of social, political and economic ideas, that the individual in contemporary capitalism relates to and makes sense of the social
world. It has already been argued that modern capitalism, with
its complex division of labour and class structure, can survive
only through forms of ideological legitimation at both the level
of government and mundane everyday experience. But if
ideology is equated with false consciousness and defined as a
closed, dogmatic system inducing passivity and a quietistic
acceptance of the social order, then its real social function is
minimal. Ideology is a living force which binds the various and
conflicting strata of capitalism into a social and historical unity,
a flexible and dynamic instrument of class domination but one
which, if it made no sense of or was not related meaningfully to
the everyday experiences of the working class, would exercise no
legitimising function at all. Ideology as false consciousness can-

not be accepted as the means whereby the ruling class legitimises its domination over the subordinate classes.

Ideologies, therefore, are 'materialised in class practices' and are defined as a fairly coherent structure of beliefs, values and reflections of the external, social world: 'Ideology concerns the world in which men live, their relations to nature, to society, to other men and to their own activity including their own economic and political activity'.[11] Ideologies, therefore, as both Althusser and Poulantzas have argued, have a real foundation in lived experience. But in attempting to relate the *specifically ideological* level within a social formation to the mode of production, these theorists advance close to the position of Adorno, Miliband *et al* insofar as they define the ideological as a one-way, mechanical process and as a form of false consciousness. An ideology, writes Althusser, is 'not a system of the real relations which govern the existence of individuals, but the imaginary relation of those individuals to the real relations in which they live', while for Poulantzas, the dominant ideology strives to maintain the cohesion of the social structure by class domination and exploitation so that 'within a social formation ideology is dominated by the ensemble of representations, values, notions, beliefs, etc. by means of which class domination is perpetuated . . .'.[12] To be sure, Poulantzas's formulation is tautologous and his general approach to the social foundation and function of ideology mechanical in the extreme: by arguing that within a social formation the ideological exists as an independent, partly autonomous structure (or level) which functions to place the agents of social processes in their social positions within the social formation, he eliminates the crucial role of praxis and consciousness in the genesis and social efficacy of ideologies. The main thrust of the Althusser–Poulantzas schema lies in its attempt to fuse together state and civil society and thus identify Gramsci's concept of hegemony as historicist. This is an important point: for Althusser and Poulantzas, the concept of hegemony as a form of 'active consent' by the subordinate strata is historicist precisely because it confers on the *subject* the means whereby the relationship between dominated and dominant classes is secured.[13] In opposition to the 'humanist' Marxism of Adorno, Horkheimer,

Marcuse and Gramsci, the 'structuralist' Marxism of Althusser and Poulantzas rejects the notion of praxis and historical subject in favour of a concept of society and the working class as subjectless, that is, the proletariat is seen as an agent of production, the occupant and support (Träger) of the objective structures and functions of the capitalist social formation. Men are the 'bearers' of objective roles and functions and thus cannot shape ideology in the way suggested by Gramsci's concept of 'active consent'. Ideology is a completely unconscious process. [14]

As was argued in Chapter Two, the concept of society as a dialectical structure of distinct but related *levels* existing in relative autonomy from the mode of production and thus developing at differing tempos (the law of uneven development) is central to any Marxist social theory. But it does not follow from this that the ideological level (Althusser's Ideological State Apparatuses etc.) is a simple, one-way process exerted on men as passive bearers of external socio-economic processes; ideology is mediated by those private institutions which Gramsci emphasises in his analysis of hegemony – the institutions of wage bargaining at the factory level, working-men's associations, political and trade union institutions as well as the institutions of the mass media. In a modern capitalist social formation, of course, the working class and its various organisations do not form a homogeneous whole but, through the uneven development of the capitalist mode of production and the contingent 'superstructural levels', a highly complex, differentiated structure emerges comprising workers in technologically intensive industries with strong trade union representation and those who work for the industrial petty-bourgeoisie often in small work units and with a history of weak trade union organisation. The working class as a whole is an exploited class sharing a common abstract relationship to the mode of production, a fact which perhaps accounts for the existence of common ideas and aspirations among widely different strata, but, as the sociological analysis of political consciousness has shown, the working classes in the most advanced capitalist industries do not have the kind of unitary ideology which the Althusser–Poulantzas model (not to mention that of the Frankfurt School, Miliband *et al*) would seem to suggest. A highly paid, skilled worker, for example, will accept the concept of 'national interest' and the widespread existence of social inequality as natural phenomena while, at the same time, believing in the class basis and class politics of Social Democratic parties. Consciousness is riven with contradictions, and the ideologies which structure consciousness at the level of ordinary, everyday experience are quickly transformed from a formal coherence into a practical incoherence. The view that ideologies are coherent structures transmitted directly as practice into working-class consciousness is misleading on two levels:

(1) the formal coherence of ideology is not maintained at the popular, common-sense level since ideologies must possess a practical content which then becomes the basis of action and understanding;

(2) the argument that ideologies are by nature 'practical-social' as opposed to 'theoretical' (theoretical being the realm of science) fails to grasp that, at the level of practice, an ideology must have some 'theoretical' content, a conceptual structure which enables the individual to 'make sense' of the social world. Ideologies are both practical and theoretical, incoherent and contradictory.

The conscious, theoretical and practical components of ideology (the function of 'making sense' and understanding in order to act) thus relate immediately to the question of hegemony and legitimation. It is not a matter of the masses passively acquiescing in cultural domination or of a monolithic ideology which bourgeois institutions manipulate to maintain capitalist inequality and exploitation, for only in a situation of 'direct domination' would such pessimism have relevance. Rather, as we have suggested earlier in this chapter, the historical evolution of modern capitalism is characterised by a move away from forms of social organisation built upon the state's dominion over civil society and increasingly towards the creation of a social structure in which institutions maintain their independence and resilience: civil society is stronger today than at any time in the past since it is only in the twentieth century that those institutions based on the subordinate class – trade unions, Social Democratic political parties – have achieved any genuine role in the framing of public policy and developed the unity and strength which flow from mass organisations. It is a perverse argument which locates a strong civil society only in a period when working-class organisations were minority institutions or non-existent. Nineteenth-century Europe was dominated economically by the bourgeois class, whose hegemony within the advanced capitalisms was becoming more and more pervasive. But with the real development of working-class organisation the contemporary problem of legitimacy and bourgeois hegemony emerges within a strengthened, not weakened, civil society. Thus the role of the mass media (the 'consciousness industry', 'culture industry' or 'ideological apparatuses') in transmuting formal bourgeois ideology into forms of practical-theoretical popular consciousness within the social context of modern capitalism is never a straightforward one-way process of 'cultural manipulation'.

What is at issue here is the relation of the mass media to the mode of production and to a Marxist theory of social formations: the law of uneven development and the concept of interrelated structural levels, suggest that cultural institutions do not reflect passively and mirror-like the economic interests of the dominant class but possess a partially autonomous character existing in a semi-independent relationship with the capitalist class. To be sure this concept of partial autonomy is imprecise but it does allow for the formulation of a two-stage model of cultural mediation whereby the institutions of the mass media transmute ruling class ideology as they simultaneously create ideology in the form of the practical-theoretical; through representations, values, aspirations the mass media transform ideology into concepts amenable to popular consciousness and it is this structure which is further mediated by social institutions and associations. As mass media research has shown, there are no unmediated effects of cultural forms; television and radio programmes, cinema and the reading of pulp fiction and newspapers are meaningfully related to the individual's existence through family networks, friends, fellow workers, and so on. Such mediations, however, are non-problematic in terms of the transmission of ideology for the whole point is that the mass media themselves form a major process of cultural mediation, their function being possible only within the context of a strong civil society. In totalitarian societies, the mass media functions as a direct support for the domination of the ruling bureaucracy or class; the mass media as partially autonomous institutions and not conveyor belts for ideological indoctrination can exist only within those societies where some form of hegemony pervades civil society. In Western capitalism, therefore, the mass media function to define the range of problems within a given situation and thus create a sense of openness and, in the case of television, 'impartiality'. Of course, the view that television (financed either by government or privately) is partly autonomous does not imply an automatic neutrality: the treatment of industrial relations conforms to a partial and ideological standpoint. For example, striking workers are usually interviewed on the picket line while the management's case is put by spokesmen interviewed in the more comfortable surroundings of an office – capital is thus related to labour in a formal equality of power. In this way, class conflict is characterised by television as inimical to the national interest and industrial relations are treated in terms of social consensus and the maintenance of the social structure; class conflict is thus seen as abnormal rather than as an essential component of the capitalist class structure; as for the causes of strikes, they will tend to remain in the background.[15] But this is not overt propaganda; television news and current affairs programmes do not set out deliberately to indoctrinate. Rather, they assume a structure of discourse, a definition of both the range and the nature of the problems, and it is this which shapes the treatment of themes and issues. To argue that the mass media fail to give equal weight to a socialist point of view on the ownership of property and the nature of the capitalist social order is beside the point: as the Director General of the B.B.C. has put it quite recently:

Yes, we are biased – biased in favour of parliamentary democracy. . . . It is our business to contribute to the debate by making available to the widest general public the opinions of those who are directly engaged in it. It is not our business to shape the end of the debate. That is for the electorate, guided by the politicians.[16]

For if there is, within civil society, bourgeois hegemony exercised over the major cultural institutions, then the agencies of the mass media must reflect, in part, the existence of a widespread consensus which, based on bourgeois ideology, is neither *forced* nor *unconscious*. At the level of popular consciousness, ideas on the class nature of capitalism coexist with the acceptance of the concept of national interest. Legitimacy is more problematic today than it was during the nineteenth century; the survival of bourgeois society attests to the strength of civil society and in particular working-class institutions which have made this survival possible. It is not the mass media which maintain contemporary capitalism.

The Crisis of Bourgeois Legitimacy: Habermas and Bell

The persistence of bourgeois ideology as a form of practical-theoretical popular consciousness is due partly to the dominant position of the bourgeoisie within the social structure but equally to the nature of working-class life in its everyday routines at home and work discipline in the modern factory – the weight of Trotsky's habits, customs and traditions. But as Max Weber has emphasised, capitalism tends to break up old ways of living and working, leading to a rejection of 'everyday routine as an inviolable norm of conduct'[17] and thus the erosion of traditionalism as a mode of political legitimation. And as capitalism revolutionises ideology so too does it revolutionise class relations and awareness. Writing in 1848, John Stuart Mill described with remarkable prescience the implicit crisis in bourgeois society:

> Of the working men, at least in the more advanced countries of Europe, it may be pronounced certain that the patriarchical or paternal system of government is one to which they will not again be subject. That question was decided when they were taught to read, and allowed access to newspapers and political tracts . . . . The working classes have

taken their interests into their own hands, and are perpetually showing that they think the interests of their employers not identical with their own, but opposite to them.[18]

Mill's conclusion was too optimistic but his understanding of the role of consciousness in legitimising class domination was acute even though he had no grasp of the social function of ideology. As has been argued above, this crisis of legitimacy reflected the transition from forms of domination based on pre-capitalist ideology to a capitalist social order in which the bourgeoisie was the undisputed dominant class in both the economic and the cultural fields. Of course, this crisis varied in intensity and in the method of resolution from one capitalist country to another but the essential condition for success was a politically divided and unorganised working-class movement. It is the second, prolonged crisis of legitimacy which develops out of capitalist hegemony. With the burgeoning strength of civil society and working-class political institutions combined with the recurrent economic crises of capitalist production, belief in the ability of capitalism to maintain and create appropriate institutions is challenged: legitimacy is essentially a question of evaluation, of accepting the legality and social relevance of bourgeois political institutions and it is in this sense that legitimacy is bound up with the practical-theoretical structure of ideology. For some writers, however, legitimacy, social consensus and social integration have become the essential functions of the capitalist state. In the work of Habermas, in particular, the problem of legitimacy flows directly from the disintegration of the bourgeois public sphere and the development of fundamental changes in the relations of contemporary capitalist production. The nineteenth-century model of a free market economy which functioned to create both capital accumulation and social integration is no longer relevant. Today, Habermas argues, the state must 'supplement' the economy by a massive intervention in the process of capitalist reproduction and thus strive to fulfil 'two basic and often mutually contradictory functions – *accumulation* and *legitimisation*'. As James O'Connor puts it in *The Fiscal Crisis of the State*:

This means that the state must try to maintain or create the conditions in which profitable capital accumulation is possible. However, the state must also try to maintain or create the conditions of social harmony. A capitalist state that openly uses its coercive forces to help one class accumulate capital at the expense of other classes loses its legitimacy .... But a state that ignores the necessity of assisting the process of capital accumulation risks drying up the sources of its own power ....[19]

It is this contrast between the non-political liberal capitalist state kept in check by the public sphere and the highly politicised interventionist modern capitalist state which lies at the heart of Habermas's theory of legitimation crisis. His concept of a self-regulating capitalist system which carried out the major tasks of social integration is historically unreal in that the nineteenth-century capitalist state quite deliberately integrated the working class through educational reforms, the extension of the franchise and, at the beginning of the twentieth century, by the introduction of welfare provisions, developments which helped in the growth of civil society; equally, the state's role in the accumulation of capital has never been neutral as evidenced by the close relation of capitalist banking and finance capital interests with the central banking system and the export of capital under the umbrella of direct state control to undeveloped countries. Nineteenth-century imperialism formed an integral part of European capitalism and, especially in Germany and France, was firmly controlled by the state. Of course, social expenditures within the state budgets have risen and the role of central planning has become more significant within modern capitalism, but these developments belong to the essential historical nature of capitalism itself (that is, capitalism as both an economic and a social order) rather than constituting a qualitative transition to a new form of social organisation.[20]

For Habermas, therefore, state-regulated capitalism (or state capitalism) succeeds in mitigating class conflict and creating a situation of class compromise within the context of the welfare state: the rapid growth of the public sector and the administrative institutions of the state has produced a transformation of the class structure from one dominated by productive industrial workers to one in which the 'indirectly productive labour power of scientists, engineers, teachers ...' forms the main basis of surplus value. It is the fusion of these two processes that eventuates in the crisis of legitimation. As long as capitalism could create a viable ideology derived largely from the self-regulating economic system, no problems of legitimacy arose, but 'because a class compromise has been made the foundation of reproduction, the state apparatus must fulfil its tasks in the economic system under the limiting condition that mass loyalty be simultaneously secured ... through structures of a depoliticised public realm'.[21] A depoliticised public sphere is essential if the masses are to be kept in order but, unlike the bourgeois public sphere, modern capitalism can create only a realm of private hedonism, of consumption and leisure. Such a sphere originates out of the need for massive planning in education, housing and so on on the part of the state, thus creating activities which challenge traditional forms of social life and modes of legitimation; total planning subverts traditional modes of motivation, especially the capitalist 'work ethic', and with the collapse of a stable middle class and rise of a mass society, loyalty to the system must be induced through 'civic privatism'. As long as the welfare state programmes 'can maintain a sufficient degree of civic privatism, legitimation needs do not have to culminate in a crisis'.[22] Habermas concludes his analysis with the pessimistic perspective of Adorno and Horkheimer: there is no group within modern capitalism capable of providing the political and cultural leadership necessary for emancipation from total administration. His model of society is a mass society in which the individual as an autonomous agent is eclipsed by a monolithic state and the state welfare apparatus.[23]

Habermas's theory of legitimation crisis is important because it reflects many of the dominant assumptions of contemporary 'radical' and 'left-wing' sociology as well as passing for orthodoxy in Marxist terms – the disintegration of the public sphere, the weakening of civil society and the drift towards an authoritarian state. But, unlike Adorno, Horkheimer *et al.*, Habermas argues that these trends are not inevitable for, if they were, there is no reason why 'late capitalist' societies should even bother to retain formal democracy. Why should the modern capitalist state not be based on ultra-conservative or outright fascist regimes in which public political and social participation is reduced to zero? For Habermas, the answer lies in the fact that the capitalist state is incapable of creating within the working population the necessary motivation: only the cultural system can provide the essential values associated with work and discipline.[24] The legitimation crisis is therefore a cultural crisis insofar as capitalist culture can no longer generate the ideology which must underpin continued capital accumulation and expansion. But what Habermas has succeeded in doing is a reification of capitalism couched in terms of the objective 'needs' of the system: the state dominates culture which in turn dominates the individual. The autonomous individual and the class struggle have been swallowed whole by the *system*.

There is little here that is specifically Marxist. Indeed, the heart of Habermas's analysis of legitimation crisis is implied in most theories of mass society and finds a remarkable echo in the work of one anti-Marxist, 'dissident' progressive evolutionist, Daniel Bell, who seems now committed to a deeply pessimistic standpoint. He agrees with Habermas that nineteenth-century capitalism exemplified a unity of social and cultural spheres in which an ethic of work legitimised capitalist 'acquisitiveness, sobriety, frugality, sexual restraint' − a sanctification of labour at the expense of immediate gratification. Bourgeois work motivation was thus grounded in the Protestant ethic's stress on other-worldly rewards for earthly activities, but modern capitalism has undermined this legitimising ideology 'by mass production and mass consumption, by the creation of new wants and new means of gratifying those wants'. The cultural justification for capitalism has become a shallow hedonism and the instant gratification of desires, a culture which has become emptied of all self-discipline, 'prodigal, promiscuous, dominated by an anti-rational, anti-intellectual temper', a 'porno-pop culture' in which all is permissible, from wife-swapping to underground films.[25] Bell concludes that:

Western society lacks both *civitas*, the spontaneous willingness to make sacrifices for some public good, and a political philosophy that justifies the normative rules of priorities and allocations in society.[26]

For Habermas and Bell, therefore, capitalism can no longer generate a viable ideology at either the level of state and government or at the level of popular consciousness. But capitalist enterprises are still as devoted to the pursuit of profit as the nineteenth-century entrepreneur whether inspired by the Protestant religion or not: legitimation problems now have less to do with the motivational structures of the bourgeoisie and petty bourgeoisie than with the ideological acceptance of capitalism on the part of the working class. Legitimation crises are not the result of the development of mass societies and monolithic collectivist trends in modern culture or of changes in bourgeois motivation but flow directly from the historical weaknesses of bourgeois-class domination. As a class, the bourgeoisie was forced to revolutionise the mode of production and with it all social and cultural practices; in pursuit of political domination, the bourgeoisie built a strong civil society in which working-class institutions flourished. In Britain, the bourgeoisie turned firstly to the working class for support against the aristocracy, then towards the aristocracy against the working class. In Germany, a strong state and a powerful aristocracy succeeded in subjugating the bourgeoisie until after the First World War. In the twentieth century, capitalist-class domination has survived through the institutions of the labour movement, Social Democratic governments and the involvement of trade unions in government decision-making: as a dominant class the bourgeoisie cannot rule solely through its own institutions but must base its authority on those alternative and opposed class institutions whose independent existence hinges on a strong civil society. In these circumstances the lack of ideology, or '*civitas*', or motivation would surely sound the death knell of capitalism itself. But capitalist hegemony over civil society is maintained by spreading ideologies which are socially relevant and flexible, ideologies which are constantly transformed by the revolutionary dynamics of the capitalist mode of production. To be sure, ideological legitimation is more problematic today with the emergence of a strong working-class movement with its political and social aspirations constantly frustrated by its own political party (or parties), but more particularly, with the real democratisation of culture which has characterised twentieth-century capitalisms. It is within this process, uneven as it has been, that the real crisis of legitimacy for modern capitalism is surely to be found.

Chapter 5

Mass Culture or Democratisation of Culture?

Within the context of theories and concepts of mass society and mass culture is posed the essential problem of political legitimation. As we have seen, there are those who argue for the collapse of civil society and the domination of the state over the modes of communication and culture, locating the causes of this development within the immanent technological superstructure of contemporary capitalism (or 'late capitalism'). As was argued in Chapter One, cultural critics such as T. S. Eliot and F. R. Leavis, while more concerned with the literary aspects of culture, equally argued that technology was the direct cause of the collapse of values and the levelling of cultural taste. In all versions of the mass culture thesis, the crisis of values and the problems of legitimacy are mechanically related to the blind workings of a technological determinism by which democracy itself is ultimately threatened. This chapter will explore the relationship between the democratic institutions of capitalism and the inevitability of a uniform, mass culture.

The Social Formation and the Concept of Cultural Levels

What is mass culture? For Dwight MacDonald, an American critic, it is quite simply a culture 'fabricated by technicians hired by businessmen; its audience are passive consumers, their participation limited to the choice between buying and not buying'. MacDonald concludes by arguing that mass culture 'threatens High Culture by its sheer pervasiveness, its brutal overwhelming quantity'.[1] In the spirit of Leavis and Horkheimer, American critics thus endorse a simplistic identification of mass communications with cultural decline: 'At its worst, mass culture threatens not merely to cretinize our taste but to brutalise our senses while paving the way to totalitarianism. And the interlocking media all conspire to that end.'[2] Mass culture thus 'reinforces those emotional attitudes that seem inseparable from existence in modern society – passivity and boredom'.[3]

In these definitions, mass culture is equated with the debasement of certain cultural standards inherited from the past in the fields of music, literature and art – a result of the emergence of art forms dedicated exclusively to the making of profit for the creators and entertainment and hedonism for the consumers. Following Adorno and Horkheimer, Leo Lowenthal argues that mass culture is characterised by standardisation, stereotype, conservatism, mendacity and manipulation and, in contrast to the 'genuine experience' of art, offers 'spurious gratification'; in the same vein, Arnold Hauser defines mass culture as 'artistic or quasi-artistic production for the demand of a half-educated public, generally urban and inclined to mass-behaviour', its social function the mitigation of a pervasive boredom, urban man's 'unhealthy dread of doing nothing'.[4] Other critics are more optimistic, identifying mass culture with democracy and pluralism, with the growth of education and the values of individual autonomy and humanism; this 'progressive evolutionist' view of mass culture generally prefers the concept of popular culture to mass culture and favours the broadening of the concept to include art, literature, music and all leisure activities based on the home and the community. As was pointed out in Chapter One, the progressive evolutionist concept of popular culture rejects the idealisation of the past and points to the increasing participation of all social strata in political and social decision-making. Nineteenth-century society was dominated by poverty, ignorance and exclusiveness with high culture triumphant and its guardians confident in maintaining their hold over society; the rapid development of technology and the growth of literacy and communications have democratised, not brutalised, the masses.[5]

There seems no bridge between these two opposing viewpoints. Large-scale capitalist production is thus the cause of cultural diversity and pluralism *and* the collapse of civil society; capitalism democratises and yet transforms everyone into a mere passive spectator. The irreconcilability of these two approaches is brought out in Arnold Hauser's comment that 'the products of mass culture are put out by the entertainments industry not to satisfy, but to exploit, people's cultural needs ... (and) the poor quality of these products is due to a historical co-incidence − of democratisation of culture with competitive capitalism'.[6] However, as this chapter will attempt to show, the real advances in the democratisation of culture occurred *after* capitalism had passed from its competitive *laissez-faire* stage to its contemporary form of monopoly organisation.

Central to these theories is the distinction between 'high' and 'low' culture. As was argued in Chapter Two, culture is forged from its material basis in the mode of production and the social relations of production and any attempt to locate different levels of culture must be rigorously analysed in terms of the social formation and the development of communications within the mode of production. But with theories of mass culture, the cultural levels, whether distinguished as high and low or high, middle and popular, are never related to a concept of society as a totality or to the mode of production; rather, a moral, not scientific, analysis of cultural structures is presented as shown in the frequent citation of a correlation between democracy, egalitarianism and the collapse of 'high standards'. Fatuous arguments (often no more than ideological assertions) are put forward as proof that the broadening of the reading habit as evidenced in the growth of library borrowing and the increase of non-fiction and classic fiction titles published as paperbacks is necessarily negated by the equally rapid growth of mass-produced popular fiction and that 'culture as a stable body of accomplishments must decline' with the tendency for culture 'to be in some sense proletarianised'. Mass culture theories based on the distinction between high and low cultural levels tend to romanticise and dehistorise the past, building myths of barely literate societies with 'high' cultures that unified the social structure since the 'standards for appreciation of high literature and art were sufficiently closely associated with the standards of . . . a social elite'. In contrast, modern mass societies, in choosing equality over excellence, have no room for creative élites. Instead, a culture emerges created for the market by professionals, a mass culture which absorbs everyone into its 'standardless world', reaching out into all corners of society.[7]

This view that the masses threaten 'high culture' as a result of democratic trends in capitalist society which eliminate culturally creative élites assumes some kind of automatic adjustment between economic change and cultural development. Of course, as the mode of production and social relations are revolutionised by private capital, both the political and the cultural structures are transformed – but not mechanically; change is uneven and contradictory as the concept of the social formation as a totality of structural levels partially autonomous from the economic structure suggests. Mass culture theory has no concept of society in this sense and therefore treats the democratisation of culture as an inevitable and evolutionary process stripped of its highly complex relationship with bourgeois hegemony and the bourgeois public sphere. The whole question of the democratisation of culture can be analysed only in terms of its specific historical determinations and development, especially of the relation of literacy and reading habits to the forging of human consciousness and action.

The Development of Capitalist Culture: Institutional Structure and the Threat from Below

If culture is defined both as a whole way of life which involves literary, artistic and symbolic modes of man's understanding of the social world and which allows him to aspire to and achieve a real sense of individual selfhood and action and as constituting the basis of the material mode of life – a definite style of life – in human communities and in work, then it clearly raises the fundamental problem of communication. An awareness of the self involves a consciousness of interests and potential conflicts as well as the ability to communicate this awareness to others. Only in a literate society does this consciousness of self and of interests relate to history and to the past; a literate culture generates a cumulative awareness of the past and especially of the notion of the present as history; the development of writing and then printing had the effect of sharply distinguishing the present from the past and thus raising the possibility of evaluation and criticism. As Jack Goody and Ian Watt have argued, in a non-literate society, 'the cultural tradition functions as a series of interlocking face-to-face conversations in which the very conditions of transmission operate to favour consistency between past and present, and to make criticism ... less likely to occur. ... While scepticism may be present in such societies, it takes a personal, non-cumulative form ....'[8] They go on to point out that, in non-literate cultures, the tendency is for myth and history to merge into one; the oral tradition is dominated by traditionalistic elements which make analytical reasoning impossible. It is only with the development of writing and the intellectual skills associated with it that it becomes possible to separate formally the various elements of the culture and thus allow for critical evaluation.[9]

The relevance of these ambitious claims to the theory of mass culture lies in the link they imply between consciousness and literacy: within literate cultures, the dominant form of communication – a form characteristic of both pre-industrial and industrial societies – is that of written records, not the oral tradition, and, if writing is the crucial factor in 'the critical accumulation, storage and retrieval of knowledge, the systematic use of logic, the pursuit of science and the elaboration of the arts', then the prerequisite for any genuine democratic culture is widespread literacy.[10] In those versions of the mass culture theory based on the myth of a golden organic past, standards of literacy are more or less ignored. And this is equally true of those analyses of the rise of the industrial working class which attribute to the workers a revolutionary and democratic potential independent of their level of literacy. Both a democratic and a radical culture necessitate a degree of literacy so that the working man can participate meaningfully in political and social activities. Awareness of the individual's relationship to the whole (whether a group, a class or a society) is mediated through knowledge that is broadly historical: selfhood, action and literacy are inseparable.

These observations, then, suggest that in discussing the development of a democratic or a mass culture two separate although related issues have to be taken into account. Firstly, that the rapid growth of a middle-class European reading public in the latter half of the eighteenth century, while dependent on new techniques of printing and the growth of the circulation library, was essentially the institutional expressions of the hegemonic aspirations of the bourgeois class and reflected the gradual democratisation and evolution of a new, secular culture. It is important not to exaggerate these trends, restricted as they were to a small milieu. Nevertheless, by the 1750s the burgeoning bourgeois media in England were firmly in the hands of capitalist entrepreneurs who produced and distributed their products on the basis of a mass circulation: *Gentleman's Magazine*, for example, founded in 1731, achieved a circulation of 10,000 – a remarkable figure in a country with a population of between six and seven million; a vigorous sub-literature built around crime, eroticism and political corruption achieved a popularity that rivalled the equally successful fictions of Fielding, Defoe, Richardson and Smollett; and finally, there was the rapid development of the press with the founding of such newspapers as the *Morning Chronicle* and the *Morning Post* between 1769 and 1772 and, in 1785, *The Times*.[11] The realm of culture was opened to a much broader section of society than ever before, thus becoming a challenge to the privileged status of aristocratic and traditional culture but far from constituting a distinctive high culture or a genuinely democratic one. Hence, the second important issue that must be taken into account in any analysis of mass culture as a historical phenomenon is that, during the course of the eighteenth century, the democratising of culture set in motion by cheap printing, libraries, newspapers and the middle-class reading public excluded the emerging working class

on both an economic and literacy basis and led to the development of what some contemporary critics would call mass
culture. Any discussion of so-called 'cultural decline' from a
high point of the eighteenth, or indeed, the nineteenth century
must take into consideration the fact that the reading public has
always preferred entertainment through popular fiction rather
than the more serious products of high culture.

The middle-class reading public was educated and literate. It
is true, of course, that the working-class reader did exist during
the eighteenth century, that sunday schools and other
philanthropic institutions provided a limited education for the
working class but it is doubtful if more than a small minority
had mastered the arts of reading and writing, especially if one
bears in mind that the emerging working class lacked the institutional culture so necessary for widespread literacy. The
bourgeois culture was based on its access to education and
libraries and, although E. P. Thompson has rightly warned
against underestimating the degree of literacy among the skilled
manual workers, it seems unlikely that the irregular education
afforded by factory evening schools and the limited intellectual
content of ballads and almanacs formed a sufficient basis for an
independent democratic culture. At the close of the eighteenth
century, for example, the radical culture associated with writers
such as Tom Paine and, later, William Cobbett, was organised
and dominated by the middle class: Paine's *The Rights of Man*
reputedly sold 200,000 copies in the first two years of publication, a figure far in excess of any other contemporary fiction or
non-fiction, and even if these and the later phenomenally high
sales are treated cautiously, there is no doubt that both the
radical middle-class public and the working classes bought the
book in great numbers.[12] But from the 1790s onwards, through
the period of repression and prohibition of trade unions up to
the 1820s and 1830s, the growth of a specifically working-class
reading public was limited largely to the self-taught artisans who
would read aloud to their illiterate comrades thus drawing them
into a form of political consciousness. It has been variously estimated that in Britain, during the eighteenth century, approximately two-thirds of bridegrooms and one-half of brides
could sign the marriage register but, with the lack of educational

opportunities, this fact in itself cannot illuminate the broader question of the number of working-class *readers*;[13] the figures for the nineteenth century are equally unreliable, ranging from an estimated adult literacy rate of 70 per cent in England to 90 per cent in Sweden and 65 per cent in France by 1850 while in 1900 approximately 95 per cent of brides and bridegrooms in Britain could sign the marriage register. According to official government statistics, by the end of the century less than 4 per cent of school children were illiterate.[14] But there was nothing of that institutional culture which the middle class had built within civil society during the eighteenth century and augmented during the nineteenth century with its ascendency to economic power. For these reasons the working-class movement was never able to create its own cultural institutions (as distinct from trade unions) while its critique of capitalism up to the time of the Chartists tended to be rooted in a nostalgic and utopian idealisation of a morally regulated capitalism. Yet, as bourgeois culture burgeoned, so the desire for education grew among the skilled, literate and politically conscious workers while, at the same time, voices were raised from the bourgeoisie and the aristocracy declaiming against the dangerous and subversive consequences of a universal literacy.

In the 1830s, magazines and newspapers such as the *Voice of the People* and *The Poor Man's Guardian* clearly expressed the need for an independent working-class standpoint and a rejection of the bourgeois press which, as part of the bourgeois democratic culture, co-existed with government repression of trade unionism, mass unemployment and poverty. By the 1840s, Chartist political classes had been set up to teach the principles of socialist political economy; the desire to read and write and *understand* outstripped the existing institutional means. In 1840, the Durham Political Union defined the tasks of education as essentially the study of history, 'especially the history of our own country, discussing its great events philosophically not as mere matters of fact, but noting their bearing on our present state, and *tracing the entire chain of development by which the constitution of society has been unfolded . . .*'[15] (my emphasis). The relation of political consciousness to historical understanding was thus firmly placed within the context not simply of working-class democracy but of literacy itself. But such an attempt to broaden the basis of democratic culture was rejected by the dominant class: working-class organisations were attacked at first by widespread prosecutions of the unstamped press which was largely supported by the working class and then through direct physical force in the repression of the 1840s. But the more important result of growing working-class literacy and political consciousness was the gradual adoption of a policy of cultural integration at the political and social level. And it is this policy of integration which posed most problems for the bourgeois class. Many middle-class reformers were insistent that the workers must know and accept their natural status in society and, even though they must be educated out of their ignorance, they should not be educated into socialism and radicalism. The view that Chartism resulted not from economic conditions but from the growth of reading among the workers and that class conflict was the consequence of 'the march of education . . . the malign nastiness of the schoolmaster . . . the spurious morality of the present day . . . and cheap libraries . . .' [16] was typical of one response to the increasing independence of the labour movement and to the fears aroused by strikes, class violence and political agitation outside the existing institutional framework. Organisations such as the Society for the Diffusion of Useful Knowledge and the Mechanics Institutes, while formally attempting to provide an education based on science and religion, were much more concerned with combating socialist economics, philosophy and political theory. [17] But imposed from above on a working class that toiled long hours at the factory bench, they were largely ineffective appealing largely to the lower-middle classes (clerical workers and the newer professions) and were more or less ignored by the labour movement. As Richard Altick comments:

However eager he may have been for intellectual improvement, the workman was in no condition, after a long, hard day's work, to profit from the instruction . . . offered. Weary in mind and body, he was expected to sit on a hard chair, in an ill-ventilated room, while a lecturer droned on and on

about the chemistry of textile dyeing or the principle of the
steam engine.[18]

Thus, the apparently contradictory fusion of science and
technology with religious instruction formed the basis of
working-class integration into Victorian society under the
auspices of the dominant class and its ideologues. Yet, at the
same time, other bourgeois ideologists were expressing fears of
the political consequences of genuine working-class literacy and
formed a powerful opposition to the development of a universal
and free library service on the grounds that access to books, especially fiction, would lead inevitably to the acquisition of
'useless knowledge', idleness and cultural degradation. Rate-sup-
ported free libraries were dismissed as 'the socialists' continua-
tion school' and 'the perfect "god-sends" to the town loafer, who
... may lounge away his time among the intellectual luxuries
which his neighbours are taxed to provide for him ...'. Such was
the confusion of intention and argument that other middle-class
spokesmen saw in a free library service the answer to class conflict and violent revolution. The historical background to the
Library Act of 1850, for example, which empowered local
authorities to finance a library service if they wished, was the
Chartist movement of the 1840s and the real anxieties aroused
by the consequent prospects of a socialist-led working class and
its potential challenge to bourgeois legitimacy. Yet, the
provisions of this Act were largely ignored by the predominantly
conservative local authorities and it was not until the twentieth
century that a comprehensive free library service finally
emerged: in 1896, there were only 334 public libraries but in
1911, 62 per cent of the population had access to a public
library, a figure which increased dramatically to 97 per cent in
1926, and indeed, the greatest rate of expansion of the library
service was the period of 1897 to 1913.[19]

Thus, the policy of integrating the nineteenth-century working
class through education and its ancillary services such as
libraries was largely a failure; if the proletariat was integrated at
all, it was not through the cultural institutions of bourgeois
hegemony. Of course, the bourgeoisie aimed to subordinate the
working-class movement to its authority and disseminate

bourgeois ideology through the independent institutions of civil society. But, whereas the bourgeoisie had built its own limited democratic culture on the basis of the eighteenth-century reading public's access to the circulating library and the rapid expansion of magazine, newspaper and fiction publishing, as a dominant class, it failed to extend this democratic culture to the nineteenth-century working class. Thus, the argument of Raymond Williams that the main impetus to the development of cheap publishing in the 1840s and 1850s was the conscious attempt to organise working-class consciousness and therefore 'control' working-class opinion must be treated with great caution since it suggests a conspiracy on the part of the ruling class and the existence of a unified and coherent policy of social and cultural integration when none existed.[20] Such an argument is monolithic in its assumptions, for the complex development of the cultural levels of the capitalist social formation suggests a multiplicity of proposed solutions and actions to what many regarded as *the* major threat to bourgeois legitimacy. Bourgeois culture is not a simple reflection of the political structure but a partly autonomous realm which, once the process of democratisation has been set in motion, increasingly becomes separated from the dominant class. The rapid expansion of the cheap journalism and popular fiction of the 1840s cannot be analysed as consciously directed by the bourgeoisie and its allies in the aristocracy but rather as the result of the structural failure of bourgeois democratic culture and institutions to provide for the emerging working-class reader. As has been argued, by the 1830s, there existed a substantial working-class reading public which subscribed to the radical press and supported radical publishing, and there is no doubt that the success of Cobbett and later the Chartist writers and newspapers as well as the popularity of and the demand for specifically working-class educational institutions demonstrate the resilience of a social class which, deprived of political rights and working and living in the most appalling conditions, nevertheless demanded *its* place within the culture. There were few libraries, the majority of workers toiled fourteen hours or more a day and six full days a week (the Saturday half-day was not introduced until the 1860s), and the high cost of books effectively excluded the working-class reader from the emerging print culture: in the 1830s, for example, a skilled manual worker might earn thirty shillings a week but the price of a reprinted novel would be five shillings while new books cost well over a pound each.[21] Thus, deprived of any meaningful institutional access to bourgeois culture and with the decline of Chartism and the collapse of the independent radical press, the working-class reader had no other alternative than that of the new commercialised popular culture.

In the mid-nineteenth century, then, a culture emerged which aimed directly at a mass market and which was in no sense a development of the radical culture of the 1820s and 1830s but rather of those earlier, popular traditions which had flourished on a much more restricted scale in the seventeenth and eighteenth centuries. Popular culture has its social basis in material production; the early ballads and chapbooks which usually portrayed in sensational terms and crude language the exploits of highwaymen and other romantic figures as well as providing details of scandal and news of the latest executions were manufactured by professionals for consumption in an urban mass market. In this sense, bourgeois democratic culture and commercial culture are closely linked, being the products of the same economic processes. Nineteenth-century mass literature evolves out of the earlier forms of popular culture but commands a greater market potential. It is important to emphasise that these trends in themselves are part of that process of democratising culture initiated by capitalist forces which the more astute bourgeois commentators noted during its very development. In his famous article, 'The Unknown Public', written in 1858, the novelist Wilkie Collins argued that:

The Unknown Public is . . . hardly beginning, as yet, to learn to read. The members of it are evidently, in the mass, from no fault of theirs still ignorant of almost everything which is generally known and understood among readers whom circumstances have placed, socially and intellectually, in the rank above them . . . . The future of English fiction may rest with this Unknown Public, which is now waiting to be taught the difference between a good book and a bad. It is probably a question of time only . . . . To the penny journals of the present time belongs the credit of having discovered a new public.[22]

The bad books were clearly the mass-produced cheap fiction such as Gothic horror novels, sentimental and domestic stories with such sensational titles as *The Death Ship, The Pirate's Bride* and *The Maniac of the Deep*, women's romance novels (which date from the 1850s), plagiarisms of Dickens with titles like *Oliver Twiss* (which ran to twice the length of the original), *Nickelas Nicklebery* and *Mr Pickwick in America*, and the vast amount of pornographic literature produced during the latter half of the nineteenth century, much of which was consumed by the literate upper classes. But in the same way as the major institutions of bourgeois culture excluded the working class so this new commercial bourgeois culture failed: as many critics have pointed out, the readership of nineteenth-century popular fiction, newspapers and magazines was always well below the existing literacy levels. In 1860, the readership for the popular Sunday newspapers was 12 per cent and it was not until the twentieth century that the readership of daily and Sunday newspapers became a mass one.[23] The evidence unmistakably points to the persistence of minority readerships for the products of both 'high' culture and the new, commercialised culture. The most highly industrialised capitalist society in Europe while possess ing the technological, economic and social structural means for realising a transformation to a truly open and democratic culture, thus succeeded in creating neither a democratic nor a mass culture.

The Dialectic of Modern Culture: the Political Consequences of Literacy and Mass Consumption

In the previous chapter, it was argued that the crisis of legitimacy for the nineteenth-century bourgeoisie arose out of its weakness as a ruling class in that its domination rested initially on working-class support against the old ruling classes and then on the aristocracy against the inevitable emergence of the working class as a potentially independent political force. Thus, the opposition to the expansion of bourgeois democratic culture was essentially political and based on fears that increasing literacy must necessarily radicalise the working class and lead to a decline in culture standards. Such sentiments found their expression, for example, in the widespread feeling that the reading habit was becoming too passive and was causing an atrophy of the intellect – arguments which, as we have seen, are characteristic of some versions of the mass society thesis.[24] The crisis of legitimacy was solved by yoking the proletariat to the capitalist economy, to the 'dull compulsion' of commodity production so that, in Marx's words, the working class became trained to subservience through education, tradition and work discipline, accepting the specific historical conditions of capitalist production as natural, not social, forces.[25] Integration through the cultural institutions of bourgeois hegemony did not exist in the absence of a widespread democratic culture or indeed of what is now called mass culture. As yet, the working class was not regarded as 'consumption-oriented' given their low wages and lack of purchasing power. For the point here is not that the proletariat constituted a passive mass but in the absence of an effective and independent working-class leadership it was impossible to resist the impress of a bourgeois ideology that flowed directly from the economic and political institutions. At the cultural level, the bourgeoisie was weak: the new commercial culture which emerged towards the end of the nineteenth century was the only, but largely ineffective, cultural mode of integration apart from religion, politics and work. There was no adequate library service (in any case, the few libraries which did exist were used mainly by the middle class), only a restricted education and cripplingly long hours of work.

The new popular culture which developed during the nineteenth century was never intended solely for the working class. It was not the urban proletariat who consumed periodicals such as *Reynolds's Miscellany* (1846), *The London Journal* (1845) and later, *Tit Bits* and *Answers* (1880), but a new stratum of white-collar workers, both clerical and professional. When Wilkie Collins wrote of the 'Unknown Public', he had in mind both the literate skilled manual worker and this emerging middle class who, in the course of the twentieth century, used the new library service and supported the popular journals, newspapers and fiction. A typical product was the magazine *Woman's World* (1903) which made its appeal directly to 'the housewife ... to ladies in shops and offices, as a cheerful and amusing companion during journeys and tea-breaks ... to busy factory workers (as) an interesting, pleasant and useful friend'.[26] If a mass culture exists, therefore, it is not the result of working-class integration into the capitalist society but rather of middle-class integration into the commercialised bourgeois culture. If there is a threat to high culture, then, it stems not from the working class but from the social strata who, through voting habits, styles of life and ideological assumptions share uncritically in the values of capitalism.

But what is popular culture? As we have seen, the concept embraces religion, literature, country dancing, science fiction, horror films, nineteenth-century folk songs and rustic lyrics etc. The main difference between a so-called 'folk culture' and a popular culture is that the latter is based on a concept of *mass* and a mode of commodity production built around a division of labour and the mechanical reproduction of cultural objects. In general, the methodological approach of mass culture theory is to emphasise consumption rather than production and thus confuse the relationship of bourgeois democratic culture with popular culture. For popular culture forms part of bourgeois culture and, at the level of production, is merely another form of the commodity which functions to mediate the individual's relationship with the social whole.

The main tendencies of bourgeois democratic culture have developed in complex and contradictory ways during the course of the twentieth century. The capitalist mode of production has constantly revolutionised culture as it has transformed social relations and political structures, creating a multiplicity of cultural levels within the social formation. As was argued in Chapter Two, the material basis of all culture is technology, science and communications, and it is in these senses that capitalism and its culture has not suffered a decline from a 'high' point to a 'low' one. Such interpretations are basically historicist, assuming an immanent total process when the specific historical development of the capitalist mode of production has been to create a far richer and more diversified system of communications, accelerating the growth of literacy and providing a greater access to print and other cultural media than ever before. Yet, while capitalist culture has not stagnated (or 'declined'), the potential universality of bourgeois democratic culture has remained unfulfilled. As in the nineteenth century, access to the theatre and drama, the concert hall, opera houses and recital rooms remain restricted to a small fraction of the bourgeoisie and the middle-class professional stratum while painting and sculpture are hidden away in private collections. Equally, that most democratic of cultural institutions — the public library — which, in most industrial societies, has grown faster than the population itself and in America is accessible to approximately 30 per cent of the population, forms an essential part of middle-class communications: surveys indicate that less than 10 per cent of borrowers are manual workers, that 32 per cent of the population never use a library and less than 2 per cent of the population read roughly half of books published.[27] These are serious limitations on the nature of democratic culture, but with the development of mechanical reproduction on a mass scale, culture has become more democratised: television and radio have made drama, music and opera more accessible (one Shakespeare play or Mozart opera is seen by more people in a single evening's television viewing than the total contemporary audience for all Shakespeare's plays and Mozart's operas); through the mass production and sales of records and cassettes, the symphony, chamber music, song and opera have been fully democratised; the so-called 'paperback revolution', the corollary of the restricted utilisation of the library service, brings the cheap book (especially the reprint) within the range of the whole population: from 6000 titles in print in 1960, the number has reached almost 40,000 in the 1970s while the number of new titles published each year has doubled between 1950 and 1970. Thus the products of 'high culture' reach a greater audience than ever before: the argument that mechanical reproduction on a mass scale necessarily creates a lowering of cultural standards is untenable for the reason that, if the *Iliad* is sold on the same railway bookstore as a book by Harold Robbins, it does not change the quality of the *Iliad* or the individual's response to it; and a Beethoven symphony remains a

Beethoven symphony regardless of whether it is sold in a super-
market or a 'quality' music shop. Indeed, the development of
mass reproduction has probably played a crucial role in
mediating between the production of 'high cultural products'
and their social assimilation. A minority creates 'high culture',
but another minority comprising the educated and cultured
strata of society either ignores or misunderstands it: one of the
highest forms of artistic culture is chamber music, which has
always remained a minority interest while the cultured and sen-
sitive patrons of public concerts have always preferred the
'lighter' works of the orchestral repertoire to such 'heavy' and
frequently incomprehensible works (at their first performance)
as Beethoven's *Ninth Symphony* and Stravinsky's *The Rite of
Spring*.

The problem of 'high' versus 'low' culture will remain as long
as the myth is propagated that it is the *masses* who, through
their homogenous consumption habits and 'low' standards, demand a uniform popular culture. The history of capitalist culture
in all its forms shows clearly that the educated and cultured
strata were equal partners with the *masses* in demanding entertainment and diversion: eighteenth-century women's magazines,
the Gothic horror novels, pornographic literature, nineteenth-
and twentieth-century women's romance fiction and magazines
were consumed with equal enthusiam by the upper classes
(aristocracy, bourgeoisie and petty bourgeoisie); in the same
way, 30 per cent of those who read *The Times* today will also
read the *Daily Express* while 22 per cent who read the *Sunday
Telegraph* will read the *News of the World*.[28] An analysis of
women's magazines published during the 1960s showed that 60
per cent of those in the top 20 per cent of the population (higher
professional, professional and middle-class white collar workers)
read them regularly while only 63 per cent of the working class
did so.[29] If the 'cultivated' and educated upper classes are
defending high standards then they are doing so in a somewhat
perverse way.

At the level of consumption no real distinctions can be made
between 'high' and popular culture: the taste for vampires,
romance and violence was as characteristic of the
nineteenth-century reading public in general as are the

equivalent tastes in television and cinema entertainment today: although crossing class lines, the fact that the professional middle class and factory proletariat may watch the same television programmes, especially modern sport, has no real bearing on the ways in which these different strata structure the social world and their place within it or decide what actions are necessary.[30] The important class affiliations in modern capitalism, the persistence of working-class attachment to Social Democratic and Communist political parties as well as the consciousness of a class society by the majority of the working class clearly indicate the ineffectiveness of commercialised popular culture to effect significant changes in social and political values.

Thus the same processes which led to the democratising of art, literature and music through the advances in technology and communications have worked against democracy. Nineteenth-century capitalist culture failed as a mode of integration but in the twentieth century the enormous expansion of commercial culture can be seen as a more successful attempt to integrate all social strata on a common, universal basis. One result is that the organisation of popular culture has come increasingly to reflect capitalist market forces and the ideologies associated with capitalism. In many modern capitalist societies, giant monopolies and multi-national corporations now control broadcasting and television, film production and distribution and publishing at all levels: the most obvious effect of these trends is that magazines, newspapers and television programmes are produced not because they make an important contribution to education and culture but rather because they are the means of attracting advertising revenue. Few magazines and newspapers could survive without capitalist advertising forming their main source of profits. Thus the importance of circulation figures since advertising rates are linked directly to them and the resultant battles for circulation between rival newspapers, magazines and television stations have led to a levelling of content and treatment, a feverishly rapid turnover of titles and programmes in the search for commercial 'success', and the emergence of cultural media whose prime function is to satisfy crude economic interests.[31]

All this, of course, might suggest a mass, not democratic,

culture. From the point of view of production capitalist culture is not democratised; marketed on a mass basis and periodically assessed by the latest techniques of market research, it echoes anti-democratic ideologies and concern with the *status quo*. In his classic analysis of English and American comics, George Orwell noted that in *Gem* and *Magnet*, the action was nearly always centred around cricket, practical jokes, school rivalry, while in the new American magazines, the focus had shifted to the cult of violence and an emphasis on 'bully worship' so that the leading character was nearly always a superman figure, 'a sort of human gorilla'. Orwell's main point was that these comics as a whole rejected the facts of working-class life by consciously focusing on heroes and life situations outside the industrial system — cowboys, adventurers and professional footballers.[32] The same is broadly true of modern British comics which depict war with images of senseless and gratuitous violence, rigid hierarchies of power and simple black and white stereotypes, especially those of Germans (the Second World War is still the major arena of conflict in war comics) and the black man. It is interesting to note that, although the German stereotype is based on elements of fear, contempt and ridicule, he is portrayed as the equal of his enemy, the Englishman; surveys have shown that in other types of comics and children's fiction the black man, whether West Indian, African or Indian, is depicted as inferior to the white man and must therefore be yoked into civilisation (that is, submission to white authority) through the conquest of his homelands. Even today, myths of empire and imperialism constitute one of the most significant structures in this form of popular culture.[33] One of the few Marxist analyses of comics shows how, in the apparently innocent world of Disney characters (Donald Duck, Mickey Mouse and Goofy), conformity to capitalist values and social organisation determines both the story line and the individual character. The social world of the Disney comic is ahistorical, non-industrial and shaped by hierarchies of power and authority by which the majority conforms to strict standards of obedience, submission, discipline and unquestioning obedience. If there are workers, they exist as rural 'noble savages' or urban lumpen criminals; since the proletariat does not exist, there is no class conflict or antagonisms, and in a social world dominated by middle-class occupations, conflict is turned into simple adventure:

> All the conflicts of the real world, the nerve centres of bourgeois society, are purified in the imagination in order to be absorbed and co-opted into the world of entertainment. . . . (Disney) has molded the world in a certain clearly defined and functional way which corresponds to *its* needs. The bourgeois imagination does not ignore this reality, but seizes it, and returns it veneered with innocence to the consumer.

Mickey Mouse and Donald Duck are characters whose actions disguise the 'repressive forces' of capitalist production and social order: in this analysis, comics are simply cultural aids to capitalist domination.[34]

A close, internal analysis of popular fiction, therefore, will tend to show its undemocratic, ideological nature. Women's romance fiction reflects similar values to those found in children's comics. Today it is a massive industry which achieves enormous sales — 25 million romance novels are sold each year with writers such as Denise Robins publishing over 150 titles with sales of over 300,000 a year. Women's romantic fiction exudes an optimistic outlook with positive heroes and heroines dedicated to conservative values and the upholding of a strict ethical code. It is a fictional universe which has no room for mixed marriages, physical deformities or ugly people; as a genre, it is highly didactic and educational in the socialist realist sense of literature as a form of social control. The writers themselves frankly admit this role, identifying their practice as an 'antidote to permissiveness', a view shared by their readers who, in one survey, agreed with the proposition that romance fiction was 'clean and wholesome without any unpleasant sexy stuff, (leaving a) sense of pleasant existence, cheerful and relaxing'.[35] The social relations of modern capitalism find no expression here: the social world of romance fiction incorporates the affluent professional stratum of admen and media men with the male role one of rampant chauvinism while the heroines tend to be governesses or secretaries to businessmen and solicitors, their role a mere adjunct to the male; less prosaically, the environment incorporates the exotic 'jet set', fashionable holiday resorts (Paris, Majorca, Rome) or non-industrial milieux such as the Australian outback. As one writer in defending the absence of genuine problems of family life and work has put it: 'It has not been the function of romantic novelists to go beyond the dawning. How sad to watch the heroine married and pregnant . . .'.[36] And finally, Barbara Cartland, one of the most successful of these writers, quite deliberately sets her fiction in the past (usually pre-1914) since for her it is that much easier to create romantic atmosphere in an era when 'virginity counted'.[37]

Women's romantic fiction, comics and other products of *mass-produced* popular culture, if analysed solely from the point of view of *consumption*, are commodities whose function is one of entertainment, information and, more ambiguously, social control. It is over this question that the whole problem of mass culture versus democratisation of culture is posed. Of course, internal analysis of these cultural commodities will show their tendency to reinforce ideological assumptions through emphasis and silence although no satisfactory evidence has ever been adduced to demonstrate a causal link between popular culture and popular consciousness: in the works of Leavis and his followers and those of the Frankfurt School, a strict homology is assumed between collective consciousness and popular culture. In these versions of the mass culture theory, the analysis shifts quite sharply from an internal aesthetic analysis of capitalist commercial culture to its assumed effects on mass behaviour and consciousness. As we have argued earlier, such a standpoint necessarily assumes an atomised society in which hegemony, if it exists at all, is organised from above.[38] But such a 'traditionalistic' and crude behaviourist model of human behaviour implied by the mass culture theory in which the individual responds passively to a series of cultural stimuli or 'messages' ignores the elementary fact that, in societies which are not totalitarian, the cultural media function through a complex nexus of mediating factors and influences so that the cultural object itself is grasped, understood and assimilated through the influence of peer groups, occupational and professional groups, family, and other social institutions.[39] It is not a question of hegemony from above (which is not hegemony at all but direct domination) but of the relation between these private institutions and practices of civil society and the ideological assumptions of popular culture itself. That their effects may be minimal should not disguise the fact that, at the level of popular consciousness (as distinct from class and revolutionary class consciousness), the products of capitalist popular culture reflect, very often in a distorted and ambiguous fashion, the conservative structure: but as was argued in the analysis of 'proletarian fiction' and in the previous chapter, popular consciousness is not a unitary structure but complex and contradictory, dynamic and not static. And it is in this extremely limited sense that capitalist popular culture functions as a mode of social integration and social control.

Humanism, Socialism and Culture

In her influential study of *Fiction and the Reading Public* (1932) Q. D. Leavis describes what she calls the 'disintegration of the reading public' from a high point in the late eighteenth century and early nineteenth century to the contemporary situation in which the 'important' writer has become isolated from the broad literate public: the modern 'best-seller' she concludes, is 'concerned with supporting herd prejudices'; for 'the training of the reader who spends his leisure in cinemas, looking through magazines and newspapers, listening to jazz music, does not merely fail to help him, it prevents him from normal development'.[40] Such an astonishing statement is barely credible but it does emphasise the opposition to industrial and technological change in the literary form of the mass culture thesis. That such a viewpoint has no validity is brought out in Q. D. Leavis's remarks on the 'difficult' and thus unpopular writers of the 1920s – D. H. Lawrence and Virginia Woolf – whose works are 'inaccessible to a public whose ancestors have been competent readers of Sterne and Nashe'. Yet, with the development of cheap paperback publishing, the growth of a free and universal library service and increasing educational opportunities – developments which hinge on technology and industrialisation – these 'difficult but important writers' have gained a more regular and larger readership than either Nashe or Sterne. The very processes of democratisation which Leavis *et al.* identify as leading to cultural decline have generated, at this level at least, cultural vitality.[41] The reading public, far from disintegrating under the influence of *the machine*, has grown in size, and in its reading habits has become more richly diversified than at any other period in history. And it is these processes which increasingly blur the line drawn by critics such as the Leavises and those of the Frankfurt School between 'high', 'middle' and 'low' culture. The hedonistic and play elements in culture are as important as the intellectual: both Rosa Luxemburg and Sartre, though highly cultivated and erudite, were great devotees of detective fiction while those who enjoy a Beethoven sonata are equally entertained by the complexities of modern football.

Collectivist trends are characteristic of the development of the capitalist social formation and its complex levels or structures, especially modern communications and cultural media. Of course, capitalism necessitates cultural levelling in the manufacture of magazines, newspapers and visual media which depend a great deal on advertising revenue for their survival; but more importantly, the democratising of culture also implies collectivist trends in making the products of 'high' culture accessible to a much wider public although, as this chapter has emphasised, at the institutional level, they remain closed. The ideal of a universal democratic culture based on the active participation of all social strata is incompatible with capitalism since as a form of domination it rests on the belief in government by élites whose superior wisdom subjugates the 'passive masses'. The myth of the mass is as necessary a foundation for modern capitalist legitimacy as is the myth of a universal, egalitarian and socially integrative mass culture. Culture, however, is more than the products of mass production but the means whereby man humanises and shapes the social world to his purposes, a praxis made possible by the constant advances in the material basis of social relations but confounded by the capitalist nature of those relations as one of inequality and exploitation. If the rich promise of capitalist democratic culture is to be fulfilled it will be under the aegis of the socialist mode of production and a flourishing socialist civil society from which legitimacy organically flows, its foundation rooted not in the myth of the masses but in the historical reality of full, democratic participation.

Conclusion

Culture and Collectivism –
Myth as Domination

In this book I have attempted to argue that the development of state and civil society within the major European capitalisms of the nineteenth and twentieth century was dialectical and therefore uneven in tempo, depth and range; the capitalist social formation is not a homogenous unity of partially autonomous levels but a contradictory structure of the economic, political and cultural, specific levels within which there are further differentiations and contradictions. Therefore, the bourgeois institutions of civil society necessarily strive to contain and assimilate the working class although this process of hegemony is never total nor its effects conscious in direction. It is important to emphasise the undialectical nature of such concepts as 'the organisation of hegemony' or 'the control of working-class opinion' since they presuppose a subjective and voluntaristic notion of the social formation and postulate a process of social integration which is largely achieved *from above* and not from *within* civil society. Equally, the concept of a specific working-class culture existing as a separate (and in some versions totally autonomous) cultural level which stands in opposition to the culture of the dominant class must be rejected as part of left-wing mythology and ahistorical romanticism. That culture can function as a mode of integration and as a locus of legitimation has been argued in previous chapters: during the nineteenth century, culture was relatively unimportant for integrating the emerging urban proletariat who, in general, was classified as a 'mob' or 'herd' and given to 'irrational' political and social behaviour unless guided by benevolent bourgeois ideals and values. During the nineteenth century, a myth of the mass was unnecessary: the working class was integrated through the workings of the economic system, work discipline and the absence of independent working-class political institutions. It was only in the twentieth century with the complete transition from 'mob' to 'mass' that the concepts of mass society and mass culture become significant elements of social and political theories and culture is defined increasingly in terms of class domination. Thus the problem of legitimacy finds its first practical and theoretical expression in countries such as Germany and Italy at the close of the nineteenth century where a strong state had dominated a politically weak bourgeoisie and where independent workers' parties emerged to challenge capitalist domination − a situation absent from the more advanced capitalism of Britain. During the nineteenth century, the concept of mass clearly referred to the social, economic and political consequences of rapid industrialisation, the 'massing' of individuals in towns and factories and the forms of collectivist theory and practice which flowed from this, but it is not until the twentieth century that the collectivism of the organised labour movement and the collectivist ideology of Social Democracy pose a real threat to capitalist domination. The masses, through their political organisations, now constitute a viable alternative to bourgeois rule. Thus the concept of mass emerges as an integral part of the dominant ideology and popular consciousness at a time when the locus of bourgeois legitimacy shifts from above to within and the bourgeois class necessarily rejoices in the egalitarian collectivism of the burgeoning civil society and welfare state. We are all masses now.

The theory of mass culture, then, is historically bound up with the development of strong working-class political and social institutions within the framework of a mature capitalist social formation. The real democratisation of culture which has occurred within modern capitalism has functioned to undermine traditional bases of legitimacy and replace them with the secular myths of the masses and mass culture. In Chapter Three the concept of proletarian culture was examined in relation to English fiction. Thus, comparing Robert Tressell to Alan Sillitoe, it was argued that these novels reflect a definite historical trend towards independent collectivist institutions and ideology while at the same time emphasising the persistence of individualistic bourgeois values within 'working-class culture'. John Braine's *Room at the Top* is also structured around individualistic values but here the notion of masses is almost identical to the denigrating and conservative usage in the social theories of Leavis and the Frankfurt School. Therefore, at the level of social theory and literary creation, the ideological concept of mass culture has been assimilated uncritically. As part of the legitimising ideology of capitalist domination, the concept of mass culture has been transposed directly into literary and theoretical forms.

There is no mass culture, or mass society; but there is an ideology of mass culture and mass society. Capitalist domination necessarily rests on many myths for it is a mode of production based on the exploitation of labour power and its transformation into a commodity: the reality of capitalism must be hidden and masked and the social relations of production turned into natural, not historical, conditions. The function of myth in ideological legitimation is to eliminate the historical basis of institutions and processes and create within popular consciousness an acceptance of the inevitable facts of class inequality and class power. Thus, the concept of mass culture is egalitarian in its ideology although, as a genuinely scientific concept, it is static and ahistorical. Significantly, its egalitarian essence contrasts with its objective function to develop a dualism between the individual subject and the cultural values embodied in commodity production. As described in the various theories and as an important element of bourgeois ideology, mass culture is the reification of human labour, a constraining and external world of cultural objects and commodities. Modern man, wrote Georg

Simmel at the turn of the century, discovers the social world as a world of external objects which appear to enjoy a life of their own, alien forces which oppress the individual because, although man initially created them, he can no longer fully assimilate them: 'The cultural objects become more and more linked to each other in a self-contained world which has increasingly fewer contacts with the subjective psyche and its desires and sensibilities'. This split between the product and the producer constitutes the essence of the concept of mass culture: the result, in Simmel's interpretation, is the reduction of the individual to 'a mere cog in an enormous organisation of things and powers which tear from his hands all progress, spirituality, and value in order to transform them from their subjective form into the form of a purely objective life'.[1]

Simmel's analysis well describes the essential distinction between the democratisation of culture and a mass culture: a democratisation of culture implies both the development of independent institutions within civil society and, through them, the practical activities and the involvement of 'the masses' since the avenues of participation have not been closed off and social change can still be effected by popular pressure. A mass culture, however, demands a passive adaptation to the existing society and a rejection of all forms of activity to achieve social change: while the democratisation of culture gives the opportunities for political reformism (one result being the creation of the welfare state) within the context of class struggle, the mass culture concept annihilates even reformist practice as an expression of working-class organisation and allows change only through the agency of élites and specialised knowledge.[2] There are also significant differences between the collectivism of a democratic culture and the collectivism of a mass culture some of which have been brought out with great clarity in the work of Walter Benjamin who, unlike other members of the Frankfurt School, advances arguments supporting the trends towards a collectivist culture.

For Adorno and Horkheimer, capitalist culture necessarily leads to social and political disintegration exemplified in an anonymous mass culture. For Benjamin, however, the basic trend of capitalist culture is towards creating collective forms of communication based on the new technology of mechanical reproduction. The basis for these arguments is Benjamin's attempt to expand Marx's theory of economic production to artistic and literary production through a recognition of the technical and mechanical roots of cultural reproduction. Thus, the technological developments in printing, radio, cinema and photography have exercised decisive effects on both the art forms themselves and the social position of writers. The art of caricature, for example, was unknown in antiquity for the only cheap means of reproduction was the minting of coins and there existed no mass distribution of products.³ Similarly with the novel: its world is industrial and bourgeois, its readers individualistic and privatised, its technical basis one of mass reproduction through innovations in printing and mass distribution through libraries and bookshops. But as the capitalist mode of production develops from the *laissez-faire* to the collectivist economic structure so the modes of artistic production shift from the individualistic to the collectivist, thus altering the social relations of artistic production. It is no longer possible to create for a distinctive middle-class public as was the case in the nineteenth century: the collectivist mode of cultural activity (mass-produced newspapers, magazines, films, records and books) breaks down the traditional distinction between author and public so that everyone is potentially a producer and an intellectual. Drawing on experiments in the Soviet Union during the 1920s, Benjamin suggests that a collectivist literary enterprise such as Gorky's projected history of Russian factories written by the factory workers themselves is now possible.⁴

Thus the importance of Benjamin's essay, 'The Work of Art in the Age of Mechanical Reproduction' (1939), in which he argues that the aura associated with great aesthetic works and which defines them as unique objects of veneration has undergone a decisive shift with the development of capitalism and the changing social significance of the masses. The emergence of the masses, he suggests, is linked with extensive changes in the division of labour, the rapid growth of urbanism and the mass production of commodities, all of which generate a secular attitude towards culture and encourage the trend towards the factual and everyday reportage in art and literature as against the specifically aesthetic. Once it is possible to reproduce on a mass basis, artistic products lose their uniqueness, their charismatic, magical properties and the aesthetic element in culture is undermined. What Benjamin is describing is the democratising of culture in which 'the contemporary decay of the aura' flows from 'the desire of the contemporary masses to bring things "closer" spatially and humanly' and thus humanise high art through the collectivist social relations of cultural reproduction.[5]

For Benjamin, then, capitalist culture contains enormous potential for the development of a democratic, collectivist culture. Undoubtedly, Benjamin exaggerates the social significance of these collectivist trends in capitalism (particularly the reduction of the aesthetic to the prosaic in art and literature through the deterministic influence of technology), but he never attempts to argue that capitalist culture must inevitably achieve the total and passive integration of the masses. In contrast, his contemporary cultural critic, Siegfried Kracauer, while agreeing with Benjamin on the importance of technology for cultural reproduction, nevertheless follows the Adorno/Horkheimer thesis and in his analysis of Hollywood films and the German cinema of the 1920s identifies as artistically and socially significant the role of the mass ornament. In the Hollywood musicals of Busby Berkeley, for example, women are used as ornaments, as decorative objects; and in the more serious films of Fritz Lang such as *Metropolis* (1927), the workers are depicted as a mass through decorative and ornamental patterns which foreshadow the mass pageants and mass gatherings which, under fascism and communism, eliminate every vestige of democratic participation. Under fascism and communism, civil society is annihilated and the role of the masses as ornament is crucially important; in these totalitarian societies, there is indeed a 'culture industry' which strives to integrate from above through the agencies of the state and to create a politically passive and manipulated mass. Here the value of Kracauer's concept of mass ornament is obvious especially in relation to modern China.[6] But when these concepts are related to contemporary capitalism they have little, if any, value. Capitalist culture is not a totalitarian system, it is not a form of domination exercised from above. The decay of the aura and the mass reproduction of high culture and the trends towards the artistic depiction of reality in everyday terms are elements of a potentially democratic culture and not the symptoms of cultural stagnation or decline.

Social myths are politically right-wing and reactionary and their social function is to conserve the structures of domination vested in a ruling class or a bureaucratic stratum. In myth, history evaporates; reality is defined in terms of the dominant ideology, as a pre-given structure of objective laws and tendencies. As myth annihilates history so too does it annihilate praxis. If culture is the means whereby man affirms his humanity and purposes and his aspirations to freedom and dignity then the concept and theory of mass culture are their denial and negation. As a myth, it legitimises bourgeois democratic and totalitarian domination; as a theory, it is vacuous, ideological and contemptible.

Notes and References

Publication details are not given for works appearing in the Select Bibliography.

Introduction

1. See Trotsky's essay 'The USSR in War' (1939), in which it is argued that 'the disintegration of capitalism has reached extreme limits; likewise the disintegration of the old ruling class. *The further existence of this system is impossible*' (my emphasis). To be sure, Trotsky emphasised the importance of revolutionary leadership in the struggle for socialism but underlying his social theory at this late stage was a dogmatic belief that capitalist economy could expand no further and thus the culture of capitalism must decline and degenerate. This perhaps explains his exaggerated praise for such novels as Celine's *Journey to the End of the Night* which depicted in graphic detail the collapse of capitalist culture into a state close to barbarism.

2. The concept 'late capitalism' is used by such different theorists as E. Mandel, *Late Capitalism* (London, 1976), and J. Habermas, *Legitimation Crisis*, who in general minimise the importance of hegemony in the accumulation of capital and neglect the slow way, historically, that the institutions of consent are built up.

Chapter One

1. George Gissing, *New Grub Street* (London, 1968) pp.

496–7. Writing of this period, Dudek argues that 'the new mass magazines, like the urban newspapers, were tailored for all classes and all levels of intellect – at least they levelled all into one homogeneous 'market' – while the magazines once dominant took a secondary place, in the periphery of culture, where they inevitably fell into decadence'. L. Dudek, *Literature and the Press: A History of Printing, Printed Media, and Their Relation to Literature* (Toronto, 1960) p. 116.

2. David Holbrook, 'Magazines', in D. Thompson (ed.), *Discrimination and Popular Culture*, pp. 181–2. Cf. F. R. Leavis, *Nor Shall my Sword*, pp. 180–1.

3. Dwight MacDonald, *Against the American Grain*, p. 12.

4. A. de Tocqueville, *Recollections* (London, 1948) p. 69. 'Among democratic nations ambition is ardent and continual, but its aims are not habitually lofty; and life is generally spent in eagerly coveting small objects that are within reach.' *Democracy in America* (New York, 1960) vol. II, p. 245.

5. F. Nietzsche, *Twilight of the Gods*, in W. Kaufmann (ed.), *The Portable Nietzsche* (New York, 1954) p. 545.

6. Ibid. p. 645.

7. Ibid. pp. 646–7.

8. Ortega y Gasset, *The Revolt of the Masses*, pp. 11–13, 49, 62, 83. The German sociologist Max Scheler, writing in the 1920s, shared Ortega's identification of democracy with cultural mediocrity. Democracy, he wrote, degrades 'life to mass psychology, the gradual transformation of a democracy of liberal ideas into a sullen democracy of masses, interests, and sentimentality'. Only 'truly cultured élites' could resist the trend towards mass society and thus preserve 'culture'. *Philosophical Perspectives* (Boston, 1958) pp. 13–17.

9. T. S. Eliot, *Notes Towards a Definition of Culture*, pp. 48, 27, 37, 43–4, 52, 60; *The Idea of a Christian Society*, pp. 33, 39–40; *Selected Essays*, pp. 456–9.

10. F. R. Leavis, *Mass Civilisation and Minority Culture*, pp. 3–5. F. R. Leavis and D. Thompson, *Culture and Environment*, pp. 68–9, 74–5, 77, 87–91.

11. Q. D. Leavis, *Fiction and the Reading Public*, p. 53.

12. F. R. Leavis, *Mass Civilisation and Minority Culture*, pp. 17–18; *Nor Shall my Sword*, pp. 69–70.

13. F. R. Leavis, *Mass Civilisation and Minority Culture*, pp. 3–5.

14. For example, R. Williams, *Culture and Society* (London, 1958) pp. 224–38.

15. F. R. Leavis, *Letters in Criticism*, ed. J. Tasker (London, 1974) pp. 44–5, 217–8; *Nor Shall my Sword*, pp. 140–1.

16. F. R. Leavis, *Nor Shall my Sword*, pp. 174–5, 84–5.

17. C. Wright Mills, *The Power Elite*, pp. 301–20.

18. W. Kornhauser, *The Politics of Mass Society*, p. 32.

19. C. Wright Mills, *The Power Elite*, p. 320.

20. M. Horkheimer, *Critical Theory*, pp. vii–viii. The concept of a self-regulated capitalism in which culture has become an independent, autonomous reality dominating the individual is a theme developed initially by Georg Simmel and elaborated in great philosophical detail by Georg Lukács whose *History and Class Consciousness* (1923) greatly influenced the Frankfurt School.

21. Horkheimer, 'Authority and the Family', in ibid. pp. 54, 80–1, 101–2, 107–8. The argument of the Frankfurt theorists that bourgeois hegemony had been destroyed by capitalist technology (the 'shrivelling of the public sphere') is echoed in the writings of the German sociologist Karl Mannheim whose identification of 'unreason' with the 'masses' and mass society with democracy and technology was clearly influenced by Lukács, Horkheimer and Adorno. Mannheim also emphasised the decline of élites within civil society, seeing in this a trend towards a levelling of culture and totalitarianism. See K. Mannheim, *Man and Society in the Age of Reconstruction*, pp. 42–4, 96ff.

22. K. Marx, *Capital*, vol. I.

23. H. Marcuse, *Eros and Civilisation*, pp. 87–9, 91–5.

24. Horkheimer, 'Art and Mass Culture', in *Critical Theory*, pp. 273, 277–8.

25. A. Hauser, *The Philosophy of Art History*, pp. 339–46.

26. Horkheimer, 'Art and Mass Culture', pp. 273, 277–8.

27. T. W. Adorno and Horkheimer, *Dialectic of Enlightenment*, pp. 143–167.

28. Marcuse, *One Dimensional Man*, pp. 59–64.

29. W. Benjamin, *Illuminations*, p. 233.

30. Adorno, *Prisms*, pp. 32, 129–30, 41. Cf. A. Sanchez

Vazquez, *Art and Society: Essays in Marxist Aesthetics*, pp. 253–65.

31. Adorno, 'Culture Industry Reconsidered'. (First publish ed in German in 1967.) In this essay Adorno modified his earlier pessimism by suggesting that individuals could resist the manipulative effects of the culture industry but only 'up to a point'. What Adorno means by this is not specified.

32. Marcuse, *One Dimensional Man*, pp. 4–5.

33. E. Shils, *The Intellectuals and the Powers*, p. 263.

34. See especially D. Bell, *The Coming of Post-Industrial Society*, and *The Cultural Contradictions of Capitalism*, A. Touraine, *The Post-Industrial Society*, and A. C. Zijderveld, *The Abstract Society* (London, 1974).

35. Kornhauser, *The Politics of Mass Society*, pp. 230–1.

36. Ibid, p. 82.

37. Bell, 'America as a Mass Society', in *The End of Ideology*. See also L. Bramson, *The Political Context of Sociology*, chs 5 and 6, and L. Bramson and M. S. Schudson, 'Mass Society', in *Encyclopaedia Britannica*, pp. 600–4.

38. L. Wirth, 'Consensus and Mass Communication'. *American Sociological Review*, vol. XIII (1948).

39. D. McQuail (ed.), *Towards a Sociology of Mass Communications*, pp. 94–5, 76. See also Touraine, *The Post-Industrial Society.*

40. Bell, *The Cultural Contradictions of Capitalism*, pp. 156, 248, 251.

Chapter Two

1. L. Trilling, 'The Leavis-Snow Controversy', in *Beyond Culture* (London, 1967) p. 154.

2. Marx and Engels, *The German Ideology* (London, 1965) pp. 430–2.

3. Marx, *Grundrisse*, pp. 110–1.

4. Engels, *The Origin of the Family, Private Property and the State.*

5. Trotsky, 'Leninism and Library Work' (1924), in *Problems of Everyday Life* (New York, 1973) p. 143.

6. Marx and Engels, *Selected Works*, vol. I (London, 1958) p. 37.

7. Marx, *Capital*, vol. I, p. 276.

8. R. Williams, *The Country and the City* (1975) pp. 48–51.

9. Trotsky, 'Vodka, the Church and the Cinema' (1923), in *Problems of Everyday Life*, pp. 32–3.

10. Ibid. p. 19.

11. P. Cavalcanti & P. Piccone (eds) *History, Philosophy and Culture in the Young Gramsci*, p. 21.

12. M. Mann, *Consciousness and Action Among the Western Working Class*, p. 73.

13. F. Parkin, *Class Inequality and Political Order*, p. 98. See also, J. H. Goldthorpe, 'Social Inequality and Social Integration in Modern Britain', in *Poverty, Inequality and Class Structure*, ed. D. Wedderburn (Cambridge, 1974).

14. Parkin, 'Working Class Conservatism', *British Journal of Sociology*.

15. A. Giddens, *The Class Structure of the Advanced Societies* (London, 1973) pp. 152–3, 285–7. For a similar argument see also C. W. Mills, 'The New Left', *Power, Politics and People* (New York, 1963).

16. P. Anderson, 'Origins of the Present Crisis', in *Towards Socialism*, p. 30.

17. T. Nairn, 'The English Working Class', in *Ideology in Social Science*, ed. R. Blackburn, p. 188.

18. Anderson, 'Origins of the Present Crisis'. See E. P. Thompson's brilliant demolition of these arguments in his 'The Peculiarities of the English', in *The Socialist Register 1965*, eds R. Miliband and J. Saville, and from a different standpoint, N. Poulantzas, 'Marxism in Great Britain', *New Left Review*, no. 43.

19. E. P. Thompson, *The Making of the English Working Class*, p. 194.

20. Ibid. p. 732. P. Hollis, *The Pauper Press* (Oxford, 1970) argues that the middle classes remained allies of the working class in this fight although she shows that working-class papers such as *The Poor Man's Guardian* defined the workers as an 'excluded' class and sought to locate the source of exploitation in capitalist production and not, as in previous analysis of taxes,

tithes, church rates, and lawyers' fees, extracted from the working-man's pocket after he had received his wages, and used to support a corrupt government and an established Church. p. 222.

21. Thompson, *The Making of the English Working Class*, p. 670.

22. Ibid. pp. 551–2.

23. See on this especially R. Moore, *Pitmen Preachers and Politics* (Cambridge, 1974) and J. M. Cousins and R. L. Davis, 'Working Class Incorporation – A Historical Approach with Reference to the Mining Communities of S. E. Northumberland 1840–1890', in *The Social Analysis of Class Structure*, ed. F. Parkin (1974) pp. 275–93.

24. Marx, *Capital*, p. 299.

25. Marx and Engels, *Selected Correspondence* (n.d.) p. 395.

26. Marx and Engels, *On the Paris Commune* (London, 1971) pp. 128, 130.

27. Quoted in T. B. Bottomore, *Sociology as Social Criticism* (London, 1975) p. 79.

28. A. Gramsci, 'Soviets in Italy', *New Left Review*, no. 51, p. 33.

29. See F. L. Carsten, *Revolution in Central Europe* (London, 1972) pp. 111–5.

30. Williams, *The Long Revolution*, p. 307.

31. R. Hoggart, *Speaking to Each Other*, vol. I, p. 28.

32. Hoggart, *The Uses of Literacy*, p. 101.

33. Ibid. p. 95.

34. Orwell, 'Boys Weeklies', in *Collected Essays*.

35. Williams, *Culture and Society*, pp. 313–4.

36. Williams, *The Long Revolution*, pp. 40; 47.

37. Williams, *Culture and Society*, pp. 323–4.

38. In both *Culture and Society* and *The Country and the City*, Williams shows how certain English writers (Matthew Arnold, Hardy, Orwell, Eliot etc.) co-operated in the foundation of a cultural tradition, a structure of feelings.

Chapter Three

1. For further details and argument see A. Swingewood, *The Novel and Revolution*, pp. 77–90.
2. Trotsky, *On Literature and Art*.
3. Trotsky, *Literature and Revolution*, p. 184.
4. Orwell, *Collected Essays, Journalism and Letters* (London, 1970) vol. I, pp. 455–6, vol. III, p. 75.
5. See on this Swingewood, *The Novel and Revolution*, pp. 40–4, 122–4 and P. J. Keating, *The Working Classes in Victorian Fiction*, ch. 9.
6. Wheeler's novel *Sunshine and Shadows* was serialised in the Chartist *Northern Star* 1849–50; Ernest Jones, *Woman's Wrongs* (1855). See J. Mitchell, 'Aesthetic Problems on the Development of the Proletarian-Revolutionary Novel in Nineteenth-Century Britain', in D. Craig (ed.), *Marxists on Literature*, who argues that these early proletarian writers suffered from the absence of an indigenous Marxism and thus 'underestimated the present and future role of the working class in history'. For Mitchell the genre of the proletarian novel necessarily includes a progressive and committed political standpoint, a view with which this chapter takes issue.
7. H. J. Bramsbury, *A Working-Class Tragedy*, was serialised in the socialist newspaper *Justice* 1888–9; Margaret Harkness wrote under the pseudonym of John Law and published three novels of the working class between 1887 and 1890.
8. Marx and Engels, *On Literature and Art*.
9. For a discussion of Gissing, see Swingewood, *The Novel and Revolution*, pp. 123–30.
10. P. J. Keating, *Into Unknown England*, p. 20.
11. A. Morrison, *A Child of the Jago* (London, 1969).
12. Orwell, 'The Proletarian Writer', in *Collected Essays, Journalism and Letters*, vol. II, p. 56.
13. F. C. Ball, *One of the Damned: The Life and Times of Robert Tressell* (London, 1973) p. 153.
14. Ibid. p. 72.
15. R. Tressell, *The Ragged Trousered Philanthropists* (London, 1968) pp. 28, 154, 389.
16. Ibid. p. 364.

17. Orwell, *Collected Essays, Journalism and Letters*, p. 57.

18. Tressell, *The Ragged Trousered Philanthropists*, pp. 46, 85.

19. Ibid. pp. 349, 526, 535.

20. On this see for example R. T. McKenzie and A. Silver, *Angels in Marble* (London, 1968).

21. Tressell, *The Ragged Trousered Philanthropists*, pp. 202–3.

22. Ibid. p. 92.

23. Ibid. p. 440.

24. Ibid. p. 494.

25. R. Roberts, *The Classic Slum*, pp. 168, 91, 17.

26. Orwell, *The Road to Wigan Pier* (London, 1936) pp. 148–9.

27. W. Greenwood, *Love on the Dole* (London, 1969) p. 148.

28. Ibid. p. 58.

29. Ibid. pp. 201–5.

30. Ibid. p. 56.

31. Ibid. p. 255.

32. Williams, *The Country and the City*, p. 324.

33. L. Grassic Gibbon, *A Scots Quair* (One-volume edition, London, n.d.): *Sunset Song*, pp. 30–1.

34. Grassic Gibbon, *Grey Granite*, in ibid. pp. 79, 101.

35. J. Braine, *Room at the Top* (London, 1957) p. 26.

36. Ibid. pp. 164, 44–5, 40, 128.

37. Ibid. p. 81.

38. A. Sillitoe, *The Loneliness of the Long Distance Runner* (London, 1959) p. 7.

39. B. Hines, *A Kestrel for a Knave* (London, 1968) p. 82.

40. Ibid. pp. 118–9.

Chapter Four

1. R. Miliband, *The State in Capitalist Society*, pp. 181–2. Emphasis is in the original.

2. Ibid. pp. 183, 236–8. See also pp. 224–5.

3. L. Althusser, *Lenin and Philosophy*, pp. 123–73. More recently Althusser has modified these views and now argues that

ideology is less a system of material powers based on and reproduced by the institutional apparatuses of capitalism but a somewhat passive reflection of deeper socio-economic-political processes. See his *Réponse à John Lewis* (Paris, 1974).

4. W. Breed, 'Mass Communications and Sociocultural Integration', in L. A. Dexter and D. M. White, *People, Society and Mass Communications*.

5. Marx and Engels, *The German Ideology*.

6. Gramsci, *Prison Notebooks*.

7. Habermas, 'The Public Sphere', *New German Critique*. (First published in German in 1964.)

8. Marx and Engels, *Selected Works*, vol. II, p. 497.

9. See discussion in A. Swingewood, *Marx and Modern Social Theory* (London, 1975) pp. 64–8.

10. Quoted in Williams, *Keywords*, p. 129.

11. N. Poulantzas, *Classes in Contemporary Capitalism* (London, 1975) p. 289; *Political Power and Social Classes*, p. 206.

12. Althusser, *Lenin and Philosophy*, Poulantzas, *Political Power and Social Classes*, p. 209.

13. Poulantzas, ibid. p. 138.

14. Althusser and E. Balibar, *Reading Capital* (London, 1970) p. 180.

15. See for example the recent study of B.B.C. Television's coverage of industrial relations news over a six-months period carried out by the University of Glasgow's Media Study Group and published as *Bad News*, (London 1976).

16. C. Curran, 'Broadcasting and Public Opinion', *The Listener* (20th June 1974). In crisis situations impartiality is bound to go to the wall: in 1926 during the General Strike, Lord Reith, then Director General, stated quite clearly that 'since the B.B.C. was a national institution and since the government in this crisis were acting for the people ... the B.B.C. was for the government ... in maintaining the essential services of the country, the preservation of law and order, and of the life and liberty of the individual and of the community'. See on this S. Hood, 'The Politics of Television', in McQuail (ed.), *Towards a Sociology of Mass Communications*.

17. For Weber's concept of traditionalism, see H. H. Gerth

and C. W. Mills (eds), *From Max Weber: Essays in Sociology* (New York, 1946) p. 296.

18. J. S. Mill, *Principles of Political Economy* (London, 1848) pp. 322–3.

19. J. O'Connor, *The Fiscal Crisis of the State* (New York, 1973) p. 6.

20. Habermas, *Legitimation Crisis*. Thus, although Habermas argues that these state-administered welfare developments were partly brought about through the pressure of the labour movement on the ruling class, he fails to take into account that the state's role in the framing of law, the regulation of the working day, control of the currency and educational reform originated in the classic heyday of capitalism – the period from the 1850s onwards. This was certainly the case in Britain which was the most advanced capitalist society from the 1850s to the end of the nineteenth century. The concept of a self-regulating economy has no historical validity at all!

21. Ibid. pp. 50–60.

22. Ibid. p. 74.

23. The concept of a society exercising total domination over those individuals who comprise it and the related definition of the social system in terms of its *needs* indicate the reifed nature of Habermas's general theory. Such views have a kinship with sociological functionalism rather than with Marxism.

24. Habermas, *Legitimation Crisis*, part II. See also his article, 'Towards a Reconstruction of Historical Materialism', in *Theory and Society* (Fall, 1975).

25. Bell, *The Cultural Contradictions of Capitalism*, pp. 135, 105–9, 21–2, 70–3.

26. Ibid. p. 25.

Chapter Five

1. D. MacDonald, 'A Theory of Mass Culture', in B. Rosenberg and D. White (eds), *Mass Culture: The Popular Arts in America*, pp. 60, 72.

2. B. Rosenberg, 'Mass Culture in America', in ibid. p. 9.

3. I. Howe, 'Notes on Mass Culture', in ibid. p. 497.

4. L. Lowenthal, *Literature, Popular Culture and Society*, pp. 6, 11, Hauser, *The Philosophy of Art History*, pp. 279, 346.

5. For a general statement of this theme, see H. J. Gans, *Popular Culture and High Culture*, and any volume of the *Journal of Popular Culture*, 1967 onwards.

6. Hauser, *The Philosophy of Art History*, p. 340.

7. M. Bradbury, *The Social Context of Modern English Literature*, pp. 177–9, 197, and the whole of ch. XI, 'High and Mass Culture'. For Bradbury, modern capitalism generates a cultural sterility in which the writer 'encouraged to be creative, yet totally unstimulated by any serious critical or aesthetic ideas that make his artistic enterprise nationally or internationally significant'. 'The Shock Troops of Modernism', *Times Literary Supplement* (15 Oct 1976) p. 1297.

8. J. Goody and I. Watt, 'The Consequences of Literacy', in J. Goody (ed.), *Literacy in Traditional Societies*, pp. 48–9.

9. Ibid. pp. 34, 56–7, 68.

10. K. Gough, 'Implications of Literacy in Traditional China and India', in ibid. pp. 83–4.

11. For details on the eighteenth-century background I have drawn on J. J. Richetti, *Popular Fiction before Richardson* (Oxford, 1969), R. Altick, *The English Common Reader: A Social History of the Mass Reading Public 1800–1900* (New York, 1975), P. Rogers, *The Augustan Vision* (London, 1974) and Williams, *The Long Revolution*.

12. Altick, ibid. pp. 64, 74.

13. Ibid. pp. 69–70, R. K. Webb, *The British Working Class Reader*, pp. 38–40.

14. See on this P. Laslett, *The World we have lost* (London, 1965) pp. 196–7, Altick, *The English Common Reader . . .*, pp. 29–30, 170–2, Webb, *The British Working Class Reader*, pp. 21–2, Williams, *The Long Revolution*, p. 187. Webb estimates that up to the middle of the nineteenth century, roughly one-quarter to one-third of the working class remained illiterate with great variations from one parish to another throughout the whole country.

15. Webb, ibid. p. 83. For the influence of the 'moral force' as distinct from the 'physical force' Chartists see Altick, pp. 206–8. On the whole complex problem of the radical and working-class

press during the 1830s, see especially P. Hollis, *The Pauper Press* (Oxford, 1970) pp. 13, 23–4, 104. Of the *Poor Man's Guardian*, Edward Thompson writes that it was 'undoubtedly the finest working-class weekly which had . . . been published in Britain'. *The Making of the English Working Class*, p. 812.

16. Webb, ibid. p. 104.

17. Altick, *The English Common Reader* . . ., pp. 188–9, Webb, ibid. p. 72.

18. Altick, ibid. p. 192.

19. Ibid. pp. 213–39, Williams, *The Long Revolution*, p. 192.

20. Williams, ibid.

21. Altick, *The English Common Reader* . . ., p. 276. See also, L. James, *Fiction for the Working Man*, p. 15.

22. Quoted in Altick, *The English Common Reader* . . ., pp. 5–6.

23. James, *Fiction for the Working Man*, pp. 59, 62, 70, 176–7; Altick, ibid. pp. 289–90, 363; Williams, *The Long Revolution*, pp. 72, 188.

24. Altick, ibid. pp. 369–70.

25. Marx, *Capital*, vol. I, p. 737.

26. Quoted by C. L. White, *Women's Magazines 1963–1968*, p. 70.

27. P. Worsley, 'Libraries and Mass Culture', *Library Association Record*, (Aug 1967), B. Groombridge, *The Londoner and his Library* (London, 1964), J. Cochrane, 'The Haringey Library Study', in *Quarterly Bulletin of the Research Intelligence Unit of the G.L.C.* (Mar 1970), B. Luckham, *The Library in Society* (London, 1971).

28. *National Readership Survey* (Jan-Dec 1973), and see the pertinent comments of Williams, *Communications*.

29. White, *Women's Magazine* . . ., pp. 169, 192, 217. In a survey for one leading publisher of women's romantic fiction, Boon and Mills, it was found that a high percentage of readers were well-educated, young (25 to 35 years) and middle-class: 'Many of the romance readers are female "white-collar workers rather than merely manual workers, and it is quite noteworthy how large a proportion are of the semi-professional or lower professional occupations.' However, since this research was conducted through mailed questionnaires it is likely that this

social stratum would be more likely to reply than working-class readers. P. Mann, *Books, Borrowers and Buyers*.

30. In general, working-class adults spend over 19 hours each week watching television while the middle and upper classes watch less than 14 hours; the average is 16 hours per week. Of this time span approximately 10–11 hours are devoted to entertainment and the rest to news and documentaries.

31. See the factual data presented in G. Murdock and P. Golding, 'The political economy of mass communications', in Miliband and Saville (eds), *The Socialist Register 1973*.

32. Orwell, 'Boys Weeklies', in *Collected Essays*. See also, N. Tucker, 'A new look at the British Comic', *Where*, Dec, 1976.

33. See especially J. Hill (ed.), *Books for Children: The Homelands of Immigrants* (London, 1971).

34. A. Dorfman and A. Mattelart, *How to Read Donald Duck: Imperialist Ideology in the Disney Comic*, p. 76. This book was first published in Chile in 1971 and reflects the influence of the Frankfurt School in its central assertion that ideological values structure the content of the Disney comic and have an *immediate* effect on its readers: if this were so it surely does not explain why so many adults, who were nurtured on Disney *et al*, voted for Allende in the two elections prior to the 1973 fascist coup.

35. R. Anderson, *The Purple Heart Throbs: The subliterature of Love*, p. 257.

36. Ibid. p. 244.

37. Ibid. p. 104.

38. For a recent example of this formulation, see S. Hall, I. Connell and L. Curti, 'The "Unity" of Current Affairs Television', in *Working Papers in Cultural Studies*, no. 9 (University of Birmingham, 1976).

39. On this see especially, J. T. Klapper, *The Effects of Mass Communications*.

40. Q. D. Leavis, *Fiction and the Reading Public*, pp. 198, 224.

41. Ibid. pp. 223–6.

Conclusion

1. G. Simmel, *Philosophie des Geldes* (1900), quoted by L. Coser in 'Introduction', *Georg Simmel* (New Jersey, 1965) p. 22; 'The Metropolis and Mental Life', in *The Sociology of Georg Simmel*, ed. K. Wolff (New York, 1950) p. 422.

2. See for example Bell, *The Coming of Post-Industrial Society*.

3. W. Benjamin, 'Eduard Fuchs: Collector and Historian', *New German Critique*, no. 5 (Spring, 1975) p. 57.

4. Benjamin, 'The Author as Producer', in *Understanding Brecht*.

5. Benjamin, *Illuminations: Essays and Reflections*, p. 225.

6. S. Kracauer, 'The Mass Ornament', *New German Critique* (Spring, 1975); *From Caligari to Hitler*; *A Psychological History of the German Film*, pp. 148–50.

Select Bibliography

Mass Society

T. W. Adorno, 'Culture Industry Reconsidered', *New German Critique* (Fall, 1975).

T. W. Adorno and M. Horkheimer, *Dialectic of Enlightenment* (Allen Lane, 1973).

M. Arnold, *Culture and Anarchy* (Cambridge University Press, 1960).

D. Bell, 'America as a Mass Society', in *The End of Ideology* (The Free Press, 1962).

——, *The Coming of Post Industrial Society* (Heinemann, 1974).

——, *The Cultural Contradictions of Capitalism* (Heinemann, 1976).

L. Bramson, *The Political Context of Sociology* (Princeton, 1961).

L. Bramson and M. S. Schudson, 'Mass Society', in *Encyclopaedia Britannica* (Chicago University Press, 1974).

T. S. Eliot, *Notes Towards a Definition of Culture* (Faber, 1962).

——, *The Idea of a Christian Society* (Faber, 1939).

——, *Selected Essays* (Faber, 1972).

Ortega y Gasset, *The Revolt of the Masses* (Allen and Unwin, 1962).

S. Giner, *Mass Society* (Martin Robertson, 1976).

M. Horkheimer, *Critical Theory* (Herder and Herder, 1972).

W. Kornhauser, *The Politics of Mass Society* (The Free Press, 1960).

F. R. Leavis, *Mass Civilisation and Minority Culture* (Heffer, 1930).

——, *Nor Shall my Sword* (Chatto and Windus, 1972).

F. R. Leavis and D. Thompson, *Culture and Environment* (Chatto and Windus, 1942).

Q. D. Leavis, *Fiction and the Reading Public* (Chatto and Windus, 1932).

K. Mannheim, *Diagnosis of Our Time* (Routledge, 1940).

——, *Man and Society in the Age of Reconstruction* (Routledge, 1943).

H. Marcuse, *Eros and Civilisation* (Allen Lane, 1968).

——, *One Dimensional Man* (Routledge, 1964).

D. McQuail, *Towards a Sociology of Mass Communications* (Collier-Macmillan, 1969).

C. W. Mills, *The Power Elite* (Oxford University Press, 1956).

W. Reich, *The Mass Psychology of Fascism* (Souvenir Press, 1972).

E. Shils, *The Intellectuals and the Powers* (Chicago University Press, 72).

A. Touraine, *The Post-Industrial Society* (Wildwood House, 1973).

Mass Culture, Popular Culture

T. W. Adorno, 'The Stars Down to Earth; *The Los Angeles Times* Astrology Column. A Study in Secondary Superstition', *Jahrbuch für Amerikastudien*, vol. 2 (1957).

——, *Prisms* (Spearman, 1967).

R. D. Altick, *The English Common Reader: A Social History of the Mass Reading Public, 1800–1900* (Chicago University Press, 1957).

R. Anderson, *The Purple Heart Throbs: The Sub-Literature of Love* (Hodder, 1974).

R. Barthes, *Mythologies* (Paladin, 1973).

Z. Baumann, 'Two Notes on Mass Culture', *Polish Sociological Review*, vol. 14, no. 2 (1966). Part of this article is included in McQuail below.

C. W. E. Bigsby (ed.), *Approaches to Popular Culture*

(Edward Arnold, 1976). Includes Z. Barbu, 'Popular Culture: A Sociological Approach', P. Burke, 'Oblique Approaches to the History of Popular Culture'.

——. (ed.), *Superculture: American Popular Culture and Europe* (Elek, 1975).

M. Bradbury, *The Social Context of Modern English Literature* (Blackwell, 1971).

J. S. Bratton, *The Victorian Popular Ballad* (Macmillan, 1975).

L. A. Dexter and D. M. White (eds), *People, Society and Mass Communications* (The Free Press, 1964).

H. J. Gans, *Popular Culture and High Culture* (Basic Books, 1974).

J. Goody and I. Watt, 'The Consequences of Literacy', in J. Goody (ed.), *Literacy in Traditional Societies* (Cambridge University Press, 1968).

B. Groombridge, *Television and the People* (Penguin Books, 1972).

S. Hall and P. Whannel, *The Popular Arts* (Hutchinson, 1964).

A. Hauser, *The Philosophy of Art History*, part V, 'Educational Strata in the History of Art: Folk Art and Popular Art' (Cleveland Publishing Co., 1963).

——, *The Social History of Art*, vol. 4, part II, 'The Film Age' (Routledge, 1962).

R. Hoggart, *The Uses of Literacy* (Chatto and Windus, 1957).

——, *Speaking to Each Other*, Vol. I, 'About Society' (Chatto and Windus, 1970).

S. Hood, *The Mass Media* (Macmillan, 1972).

——, *A Survey of Television* (Heinemann, 1967).

J. Huizinga, *Homo Ludens* (Paladin, 1970).

L. James, *Fiction for the Working Man* (Penguin Books, 1974).

P. J. Keating, *The Working Classes in Victorian Fiction* (Routledge, 1971).

—— (ed.), *Into Unknown England* (Collins, 1976).

L. Lowenthal, *Literature, Popular Culture and Society* (Prentice-Hall, 1961).

D. MacDonald, *Against the American Grain* (Gollancz, 1962).

D. MacQuail (ed.), *Sociology of Mass Communications* (Penguin Books, 1972).

P. H. Mann, *Books, Borrowers and Buyers* (Deutsch, 1970).

P. H. Mann and J. L. Burgoyne, *Books and Reading* (Deutsch, 1969).

M. McLuhan, *The Gutenberg Galaxy* (Routledge, 1962).

——, *Understanding Media* (Routledge, 1964).

G. Orwell, 'Boys Weeklies', in *Collected Essays* (Heinemann, 1961).

B. Rosenberg and D. M. White (eds), *Mass Culture: The Popular Arts in America* (The Free Press, 1957). Articles by D. MacDonald, B. Rosenberg and Irving Howe.

D. Thompson (ed.), *Discrimination and Popular Culture* (Heinemann, 1974).

R. K. Webb, *The British Working Class Reader* (Allen and Unwin, 1955).

C. L. White, *Women's Magazines, 1963–1968* (Michael Joseph, 1970).

R. Williams *Communications* (Chatto and Windus, 1966).

——, *Television, Technology and Cultural Form* (Collins, 1974).

——, *The Long Revolution* (Penguin Books, 1965).

P. Worsley, 'Libraries and Mass Culture', *Library Association Record* (Aug 1967).

Marxism and Culture

T. W. Adorno, 'Correspondence with Walter Benjamin', *New Left Review*, no. 81 (1973).

——, *Philosophy of Modern Music* (Seabury Press, 1973).

W. Benjamin, *Charles Baudelaire: A Lyric Poet in the Era of Capitalism* (New Left Books, 1973).

——, *Illuminations* (Cape, 1970). Contains the important essay 'The Work of Art in the Age of Mechanical Reproduction'.

——, *Understanding Brecht* (New Left Books, 1972).

J. Berger, *Selected Essays and Articles* (Penguin Books, 1972).

——, *Ways of Seeing* (Penguin Books, 1972).

B. Brecht, 'Against George Lukács', *New Left Review*, no. 84 (1974).

——, 'Special Number: Brecht and the Revolutionary Cinema', in *Screen* (Summer, 1974).

D. Craig, 'Marxism and Popular Culture', in Bigsby (ed.), *Approaches to Popular Culture*, op. cit.

——, *The Real Foundations: Literature and Social Change* (Chatto and Windus, 1973).

—— (ed.), *Marxists on Literature* (Penguin Books, 1975).

T. Eagleton, *Criticism and Dogmatism* (New Left Books, 1976).

L. Goldmann, *Marxisme et Sciences Humaines* (Gallimard, 1970).

——, *The Hidden God* (Routledge, 1964).

A. Gramsci, *Prison Notebooks* (Lawrence and Wishart, 1971). See also *History, Philosophy and Culture in the Young Gramsci*, edited by P. Cavalcanti and P. Piccone (Telos Press, 1975).

F. D. Klingender, *Art and the Industrial Revolution* (Paladin, 1972).

S. Kracauer, *From Caligari to Hitler: A Psychological History of the German Film* (Princeton University Press, 1971).

——, 'The Mass Ornament', *New German Critique* (Spring, 1975).

A. L. Lloyd, *Folk Song in England* (Paladin, 1974).

H. Marcuse, 'Art and Revolution', in *Counter-revolution and Revolt* (Allen Lane, 1972).

K. Marx, *Grundrisse* (tr. M. Nicolaus, Penguin Books, 1973).

K. Marx and F. Engels, *On Literature and Art* (International Publishers, 1947).

G. Plekhanov, *Art and Social Life* (Lawrence and Wishart, 1953).

A. Swingewood, 'Marxist Approaches to the Study of Literature', in J. Routh and J. Wolf (eds), *Sociological Review Monograph*, (Keele University, 1977).

——, *The Novel and Revolution* (Macmillan, 1975).

L. Trotsky, *Literature and Revolution* (Russell and Russell, 1957).

——, *On Literature and Art* (Pathfinder Press, 1970).

——, *Problems of Everyday Life* (Monad, 1973).

A. Vazquez, *Art and Society: Essays in Marxist Aesthetics* (Merlin Press, 1974).

R. Williams, 'Base and Superstructure in Marxist Cultural Theory', *New Left Review*, no. 82 (1973).

——, *Keywords: A Dictionary of Culture and Society* (Collins, 1976).

——, *The Country and the City* (Paladin, 1975).

Culture and Class Domination

L. Althusser, *Lenin and Philosophy* (New Left Books, 1971).

P. Anderson, 'Components of the National Culture', in R. Blackburn and A. Cockburn (eds), *Towards Socialism* (Collins, 1965).

H. Braverman, *Labour and Monopoly Capital* (Monthly Review Press, 1974).

A. Dorfman and A. Mattelart, *How to Read Donald Duck: Imperialist Ideology in the Disney Comic* (International General, 1975).

H. M. Enzensberger, 'Constituents of a Theory of the Media', *New Left Review*, no. 64 (1970).

——, *The Consciousness Industry* (Seabury Press, 1975).

A. Gramsci, 'Soviets in Italy', *New Left Review*, no. 51 (1968).

J. Habermas, *Legitimation Crisis* (Heinemann, 1976).

——, 'The Public Sphere', *New German Critique* (Fall, 1974).

P. Hollis, *The Pauper Press* (Oxford University Press, 1970).

J. Klapper, *The Effects of Mass Communications* (The Free Press, 1960).

S. Mallet, *The New Working Class* (Spokesman Books, 1975).

M. Mann, *Consciousness and Action among the Western Working Class* (Macmillan, 1973).

G. Murdock and P. Golding, 'The Political Economy of Mass Communications', in R. Miliband and J. Saville (eds), *The Socialist Register 1973* (Merlin Press, 1974).

R. Miliband, *The State in Capitalist Society* (Weidenfeld, 1968).

T. Nairn, 'The English Working Class', in R. Blackburn (ed.), *Ideology in Social Science* (Collins, 1972).

F. Parkin, *Class Inequality and Political Order* (Paladin, 1972).

——, 'Working Class Conservatives', *British Journal of Sociology*, no. 17 (1967).

N. Poulantzas, *Political Power and Social Classes* (New Left Books, 1973).

R. Roberts, *The Classic Slum* (Penguin Books, 1973).

T. Schroyer, *The Critique of Domination* (Brazillier, 1974).

A. Smith, *The Shadow in the Cave: The Broadcaster, the Audience and the State* (Quartet Books, 1976).

E. P. Thompson, *The Making of the English Working Class* (Gollancz, 1963).

——, 'The Peculiarities of the English', in R. Miliband and J. Saville (eds), *The Socialist Register 1965* (Merlin Press, 1965).

——, 'Time, Work-Discipline and Industrial Capitalism', *Past and Present*, no. 38 (1967).

J. Westergaard and H. Ressler, *Class in a Capitalist Society* (Heinemann, 1975).

Index